GW00778029

HIT
SESSION
Keyboard

Liederauswahl: Bosworth Music GmbH
Covergestaltung: Agentur Glücklicher Montag

BOE7558
ISBN 978-3-86543-666-5

Printed in the EU.

www.bosworth.de

Bosworth Edition
The Music Sales Group

INHALT

36 GRAD
2RAUMWOHNUNG

♩ = 126 | 8-Beat

Leadsound: Flute

Musik & Text: Thomas Eckart, Inga Humpe, Peter Plate, Ulf Leo Sommer
© Copyright by Partitur Musikverlag / It Work Inga Humpe Tommi Eckart / Arabella Musikverlag GmbH
(Universal Music Publishing Group Germany). Alle Rechte für Deutschland, Österreich, Schweiz.

Ah,_____ ah.

Guck mal was die Jungs da hin - ten tun,__ und sag ih - nen, das will ich___

auch. Denn im - mer wie - der wenn die Jungs das tun, dann

merk ich,__ was ich brauch.__ Ich geb dir ein Ge - schenk, mach

__ es bit - te auf. Be - stell mir ein Ge - tränk, ich komm__ mal zu euch rauf. O - der

kommt ihr zu mir run - ter, ich will eu - re Zim - mer__ sehn. Wir

lie - gen vor der Mi - ni - bar,__ komm lass uns ba - den gehn. Sechs - und - drei - ßig

4

Grad und es wird noch hei - ßer. Mach den Beat nie wie - der lei -

- ser. Sechs - und - drei - ßig Grad, kein Ven - ti - la - tor.__ Das

Le - ben kommt mir gar nicht hart__ vor.__ Sechs - und - drei - ßig Grad,_____

ah.__ Sechs - und - drei - ßig Grad,_____ ah.

Guck mal, was die wie-der da hin-ten tun.__ Ich weiß__ nicht, was das soll, a-ber ich find's

gut. Al - le Jungs sin-gen und tan-zen hier.__ Kommt Girls,__ da sind wir.__

__ Schu-he aus,__ Bi - ki - ni an.__ Wir ge-hen raus. Es fängt zu

reg-nen an.__ Und wir tan-zen und kön-nen schon die Son-ne wie-der sehn, und

D.S. al CODA

jetzt 'nen Re-gen-bo-gen. Wow,__ ist das schön.__ Sechs - und - drei - ßig

Hier Jungs, da Girls, wei - ter, wei - ter, wei - ter, gebt al - les und mehr als ihr könnt.

5

AFTER AFTERALL
WILLIAM FITZSIMMONS

♩ = 68 | (no drums)

Leadsound: Piano

Musik & Text: William Fitzsimmons
© 2009 William Fitzsimmons Music. Mit freundlicher Genehmigung der Bosworth Music GmbH, Berlin.

ALEJANDRO
LADY GAGA

Musik & Text: Stefani Germanotta & RedOne
© Copyright 2009 House Of Gaga Publishing Incorporated / Songs Of RedOne / Sony/ATV Songs LLC, USA.
Sony/ATV Music Publishing.
All Rights Reserved. International Copyright Secured.

♩ = 100 | Disco-Beat

Leadsound: Flute

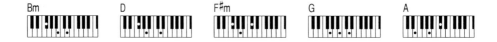

(I know that we are young and I know you may love me but I just can't be with you like this anymore, Alejandro.)

She's got both hands in her po - ckets_ and she
bro - ken,_ she's just a ba - by. But her

__ won't look at you,_ won't look at you._____ She hides true love, en su bol - sil -
boy - friend's like a dad,_ just like a dad._____ All those flames that_ burned be - fore

- lo.__ She's got a ha - lo 'round her fin - ger a - round you._____
__ him__ now_ he's gonna fight the fight,_ gonna cool the bad._____

You know that I love you, boy, hot like Me - xi - co,_ re - joice. At this point I got - ta choose, noth-

-ing to lose. Don't call my name,___ don't call my name,___ A - le -

-jan - dro.__ I'm not your babe,__ I'm not your babe,__ Fer - nan - do.__ Don't wan - na kiss,

__ don't wan - na touch,_ just smoke one ci - ga - rette__ and hush. Don't call my name,

__ don't call my name,__ Ro - ber - to.__ A - le - jan - dro,_ A - le - jan - dro.__

A - le - A - le - jan - dro, A - le - A - le - jan - dro.__ A - le - jan - dro,_ A - le - jan - dro.__

A - le - A - le - jan - dro, A - le - A - le - jan - dro.___

She's not __ Don't both - er me,__ don't both - er me,__

A - le - jan - dro. Don't call my name,__don't call my name, bye Fer - nan - do. I'm not your babe,

__ I'm not your babe, A - le - jan - dro. Don't wan - na kiss,__ don't wan - na touch,__ Fer-

D.S. al CODA

nan - do.__ Don't call my name, ___ A - le - jan - dro.__

9

ALL OVER THE WORLD
PET SHOP BOYS

♩= 130 | 8 Beat

Leadsound: Vibraphon

Musik & Text: Chris Lowe & Neil Tennant

ALL THE LOVERS
KYLIE MINOGUE

♩ = 120 | Disco-Beat

Leadsound: Vibraphone

Musik & Text: Mima Stilwell & Jim Eliot
© Copyright 2010 Sony/ATV Music Publishing.
All Rights Reserved. International Copyright Secured.

Dance. It's all I wan-na do___ so won't you dance. I'm

Feel. Can't you see there's so___ much here to feel.

stand-ing here with you,___ why won't you move. I'll

Deep in-side your heart___ you know I'm real.

get in-side___ your groove 'cause I'm on fi-re, fi-re, fi-re, fi-re. It

Can't you see___ that this___ is go-ing high-er, high-er, high-er, high-er.

hurts when you get too close, but ba-by it hurts. If

Breathe. I know you find it hard___ but ba-by breathe.

love is real-ly good___ you just want more.

Ly-ing next to me___ it's all you need.

E-ven if it throws you to the fi-re, fi-re, fi-re. All the

And I'll take you there,___ I'll take you high-er, high-er, high-er.

lov - ers that have gone be - fore. They don't com -

- pare to you, don't be runn - ing.

Just give me a lit - tle bit more. They don't com - pare, all the

lov - ers. *FINE* Dance. It's all I wan - na do so won't you

dance. I'm stand - ing here with you, why won't you move.

Ev - en if it throws you to the fi - re, fi - re, fi - re, fi - re.

D.S. al FINE

All the

13

ALL THIS TIME
MARIA MENA

♩ = 66	Pop Beat
Leadsound: Oboe	

Musik: Martin Sjoelie, Maria Mena / Text: Maria Mena
© by EMI Music Publishing Norway AS. Rechte für Deutschland, Österreich, Schweiz und Osteuropa (außer Baltikum):
EMI Music Publishing Gemany GmbH, Hamburg.

G   Bm   Am   C   Em

You self - des - truc - tive___ lit - tle girl,___ pick your - self up,

_ don't blame the world. So you screwed up,___ but you're gon - na be o -

- k.___ Now call your boy - friend___ and a - po - lo - gize,
Think all the mean girls___ that pulled your hair,

you pushed him pret - ty far a - way last night. He real - ly loves you,
are bare - foot now and preg - nant there. And you write pop songs

_ you just don't al - ways love your - self.___ And
_ and went to tra - vel round the___ world.___

all this time, oh,_____ all this time, you've had it in you,_____

14

just some-times need a push. All this time, oh,_____

all this time, you've had it in you,_____ just some-times need a

push. push.

So you've had some de-tours,__ some stu-pid men, now we know what not__

__ to do a-gain. Be-sides, you looked out,__ fi - nal-ly.__

And All this time, oh,_____ all this time, you've had it

in you,_____ just some-times need a push.

ALMOST LOVER
A FINE FRENZY

♩ = 60	Ballad
	Leadsound: Piano

Musik & Text: Alison Sudol

Your fin-ger-tips a-cross my skin, the palm trees sway-ing in the wind. Im-a-ges.

You sang me span-ish lul-la-bies,— the sweet-est

sad-ness in your eyes. Clev-ver trick.— Well, I'd

nev-er want— to see you un-hap-py.— I thought you'd want the same for me.

Good-bye,— my al-most lov-er. Good-bye,— my hope-less dream.

I'm try-ing not to think a-bout— you. Can't— you just let me be.

So long,— my luck-less ro-mance. My back— is turned on you.—

Should-a known you'd bring me heart-ache. Al-most lov-ers al-ways do.—

We walked a-long a crow-ded street, you took my hand and danced with me.— I-ma-

-ges._____ And when you

left you kissed my lips, you told me you would ne - ver, ne - ver for - get, these i - ma -

- ges.__ Well, I'd

D.S. al CODA

I can not__ go to the o -

cean. I can not drive the streets at night. I can not__ wake up in the morn -

ing, with - out you on my mind.__ So you're gone_ and I'm haun - ted, and I'll bet you're just

fine._ Did I make it that_ eas - y to walk, right in and out of my life._____

Good - bye,_____ my al - most lov - er. Good - bye,__ my hope - less dream.

I'm try - ing not to think a - bout_ you. Can't_ you just let me be.__

So long,_____ my luck - less ro - mance. My back__ is turned on you.__

Should - a known you'd bring me heart - ache. Al - most lov - ers al - ways do.__

17

AROUND THE WORLD
A.T.C.

♩ = 132	Disco Beat
Leadsound: Vibraphone	

Musik & Text: Alex Christensen, Antonio Nunzio Catania
© Ed. Scales, Ed.Akinna / Edition Alex C der EMI Music Publishing Germany GmbH.

The

kis-ses of the sun   were sweet, I did-n't blink. I let it in my eyes
ra-dio play-ing songs,   that I have nev-er heard. I don't know what to say,

like an ex-o-tic dream. The   la la la la la,____   it goes a-round the world. Just
oh, not an-oth-er word. Just

la la la la la,____   it's all a-round the world. Just la la la la la,____

and ev-'ry-bo-dy sing-ing. La la la la la____   and now the bells are ring-ing.

La la la la la.____ La la la la la la la. La la la la la.____ La la la la la la la.

In-

-side an emp-ty room   my in-spi-ra-tion flows. Now wait to hear the tune
now the night is gone,   still it goes on and on. So deep in-side of me

a-round my head it goes. The ma-gic me-lo-dy   you want to sing with me. Just
I long to set it free. I don't know what to do, just can't ex-plain to you. I

D.S. al CODA

la la la la la,   the mu-sic is the key. And
don't know what to say, oh, not an-oth-er word, just

La la la la la,___   it goes a-round the world. Just

la la la la la,___   it's all a-round the world. Just la la la la la,___

and ev-'ry-bo-dy sing-ing. La la la la la___   and now the bells are ring-ing.

4x

La la la la la.___ La la la la la la la. La la la la la.___   La la la la la la la.

rep. ad lib.

19

ALLES ROT
SILLY

♩ = 80 | 8-Beat
Leadsound: Guitar

Musik: Anna Loos Liefers, Rüdiger Barton, Uwe Hassbecker, Hans Jürgen Reznicek / Text: Werner Karma
© Valicon Songs oHG/ EMI Songs Musikverlag GmbH/Edition Undercover der EMI Music Publishing Germany GmbH / Manuskript.

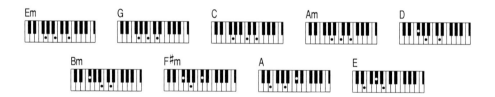

Fin - de dei - ne Schlüs - sel, 'n letz - ten Lie - es - brief.___ Wuss - te gar nicht, dass

___ du schreibst les und heul mich schief.___ Schö - ner Text, han - delt von Ge - füh - len,

von 'ner Kind - frau, halb so alt wie wir. Von 'ner Fee, 'ner un - be - rühr - ten, zar - ten.

Fühlst dich nicht mehrjung ge - nug mit mir. In mir drin ist al - les rot, das Ge - gen - teil von tot. Mein Herz,

es schlägt sich noch ganz gut. In mir drin ist al - les rot und du bist ein I - diot, mein Freund.___ Du___ ver - schmähst mein sü - ßes Blut.

Du möch - test e - wig le - ben, du wirst der Ers - te sein.___

Du luchst ihr ih - re Ju - gend ab___ und reibst dich da - mit ein.___ Geh zum Him - mel und mach dir nicht die Mü - he dich, mit letz - ter Lie - be um - zu - schaun.

Wer sein Glück nur in der Fer - ne fin - det, der muss ein - fach durch durch vie - le Frau'n. In mir drin ist al - les rot, das Ge - gen - teil von tot. Mein Herz,___ es schlägt sich noch ganz gut. In mir drin ist al - les rot und du bist ein I - diot, mein Freund.

1. ___ Du___ ver - schmähst mein sü - ßes Blut. In mir

2. ___ Du___ ver - schmähst mein sü - ßes Blut.

Al - le Lie - be der Welt, __ wenn dir __ das ge - fällt, __ vie - le Fin - ger soll'n nach __ dir fas - sen.

Dich zer - rei - ßen vor Lust __ und von all dei - nem Frust, __ dei - ner Lee - re nichts ü -

- brig las - sen. In mir drin ist al - les rot, das

Ge - gen - teil von tot. Mein Herz, __ es schlägt sich noch ganz gut. In mir

drin ist al - les rot und du bist ein I - diot, mein Freund. __

In mir drin ist al - les rot, das

Ge - gen - teil von tot. Mein Herz, __ es schlägt sich noch ganz gut. In mir

drin ist al - les rot und du bist ein I - diot, mein Freund. __ Du __ ver -

schmähst mein sü - ßes Blut. In mir drin ist al - les rot, das Ge - gen - teil von tot. Mein Herz. __

22

BODIES
ROBBIE WILLIAMS

♩ = 95 | Pop-Beat
Leadsound: Saxophone

Musik & Text: Craig Russo & Brandon Christy
© Copyright Seedpod Music / Brandon Christy Productions.
Kobalt Music Publishing Limited.
All Rights Reserved. International Copyright Secured.

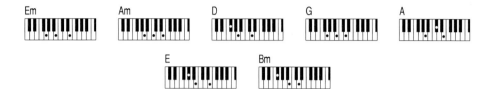

God gave me the sun-shine, then showed me my life-line.___ I was told it was all mine, then I got laid on the lay-line.___ What a day, what a day,___ and your Je-sus real-ly died_ for me. And then Je-sus real-ly tried_ for me.

U-K and en-tro-py,___ I feel like it's fuck-ing me. Wan-na feed off the e-ner-gy, love liv-ing like a de-i-ty. What a day, one day,___ and your Je-sus real-ly died_ for me. I guess Je-sus real-ly tried_ for me.

Bod-ies in the bod-hi tree,— bod-ies mak-ing chem-is-try. Bod-ies on my fam-i-ly,

bod-ies in the way of me.— Bod-ies in the cem-e-tery,— and that's the way it's gon-na be.

All we've ev-er wan - ted is to look good na - ked, hope that some-one can take

— it.— God save me re-jec - tion from my re-flec - tion, I want per-fec -

- tion.— Pray-ing for the rap-ture, cause it's

stran-ger gett-ing stran-ger. And ev-'ry-thing's con-ta-gious, it's the mo-dern mid-dle a-ges.

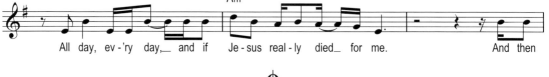

All day, ev-'ry day,— and if Je-sus real-ly died— for me. And then

D.S. al CODA

Je-sus real-ly tried for me.

BACK TO BLACK
AMY WINEHOUSE

♩ = 123	8-Beat
	Leadsound: Flute

Musik & Text: Mark Ronson, Amy Winehouse
© 2006 EMI Music Publishing Limited, London. Reproduced by permission of International Music Publications Limited
(a trading name of Faber Music Limited).
All Rights Reserved.

BAD INFLUENCE

PINK

♩= 138	Shuffle
Leadsound: Synth Lead	

Musik & Text: Alecia Moore, Robin Mortensen Lynch, Niklas Jan Olovson, Butch Walker
© by Pink Inside Publishing / EMI Blackwood Music Incorporation / I Eat Publishing For Breakfast / EMI April Music Incorporation.
Rechte für Deutschland, Österreich, Schweiz und Osteuropa (außer Baltikum): EMI Music Publishing Gemany GmbH /
Sony/ATV Music Publishing (UK) Limited / Universal Music Publishing GmbH.

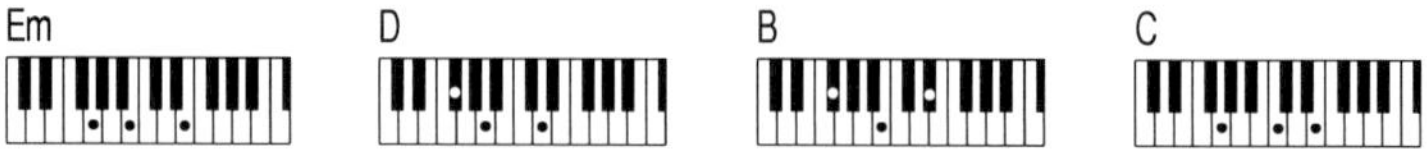
Em
D
B
C

Da da da__ da da___ da da da da da da da da da da da da da_
__ da da da da.___ Al - right Sir, sure I'll have an - oth - er one, it's
ear - ly. Three o - lives, shake it up, I like it dir - ty. Te - qui - la for my friend it makes her
flir - ty. Trust me. I'm the in - sti - ga - tor of un - der - wear show - ing up here and there,
uh oh (oh no). I'm al - ways on a mis - sion from the get go (get go). So
what if it's on - ly one o'-clock in the af - ter - noon. It's nev - er too soon to send out all the in - vi - ta - tions
to the last night of your life. Lord - y Lord - y Lord - y I can't help it, I like to par - ty, it's ge-
-ne - tic. It's e - lec - tri - fy - ing. Wind me up and watch me go, where she stops no - bod - y knows a

29

BLUE MONDAY
NEW ORDER

♩ = 130 | Disco Beat

Leadsound: Synth Lead

Musik & Text: Steven Morris, Peter Hook, Bernard Sumner & Gillian Gilbert
© 1982 Be Music / Warner/Chappell Music Limited, London. Reproduced by permission of Faber Music Limited.
All Rights Reserved.

(play accents ad lib.)

How does it feel___ to treat me like you do.___ When you've laid your hands up - on___ me and told me who you are. I thought I was mis - ta - ken, I thought I heard your words.___ Tell me how do I feel,___ tell me now how do I feel. ___ Those who came be - fore___ me lived through their vo - ca - tions. From the

past un-til com-ple - tion they'll turn a - way_ no more._ And I still find it so_

_ hard to say what I need to say._ But I'm quite sure that you'll tell_ me just how

I should feel to - day._

I see a ship in the har-

- bor, I can and_ shall o - bey._ But if it was-n't for your mis-for-tunes

_ I'd be a hea-ven-ly per-son to - day._ And I thought I was mis-ta-

- ken. I thought I heard you speak._ Tell me how do I feel,_ tell me

now how should I feel._ Now I stand here wait - ing.

I thought I told you to leave

_ me while I walked down to the beach._ Tell me how does it feel_

_ when your heart grows cold._

BORN THIS WAY
LADY GAGA

♩ = 124 | 8-Beat
Leadsound: Organ

Musik & Text: Stefani Germanotta, Jeppe Laursen, Fernando Garibay & Paul Blair
© Copyright 2011 Sony/ATV Music Publishing (85%)/Warner/Chappell Music Limited (7.5%)/Copyright Control (7.5%).
All Rights Reserved. International Copyright Secured.

(It doesn't matter if you love him, or capital H-I-M.
Just put your paws up 'cause you were born this way, baby.)

My ma-ma told me when I____ was young__ we are all born su-per-stars.
Give your-self pru-dence and love__ your friends, sub-way kid, re-joice the truth.

____ She rolled my hair and put my lip-stick on____ I must
____ In the re-li-gion of the in-se-cure____ I must

in the glass of her bou-doir.____ "There's noth-in' wrong with lov-in'
be my-self, re-spect my youth.____ A diff-'rent lov-er is

who you are" she said, "'Cause He made you per-fect, babe".____
not a sin____ be-lieve ca-pi-tal H-I-M.

"So hold your head up, girl and you'll go__ far,__ lis-ten to me when I say".
I love my life, I love this re-cord__ and__ mi a-more vo-le fe yah.__

____ I'm beau-ti-ful in my way,__ 'cause God makes no mis-takes. I'm on the

right track, ba-by I was born__ this way.__ Don't hide your-self in re-gret,__ just love your-

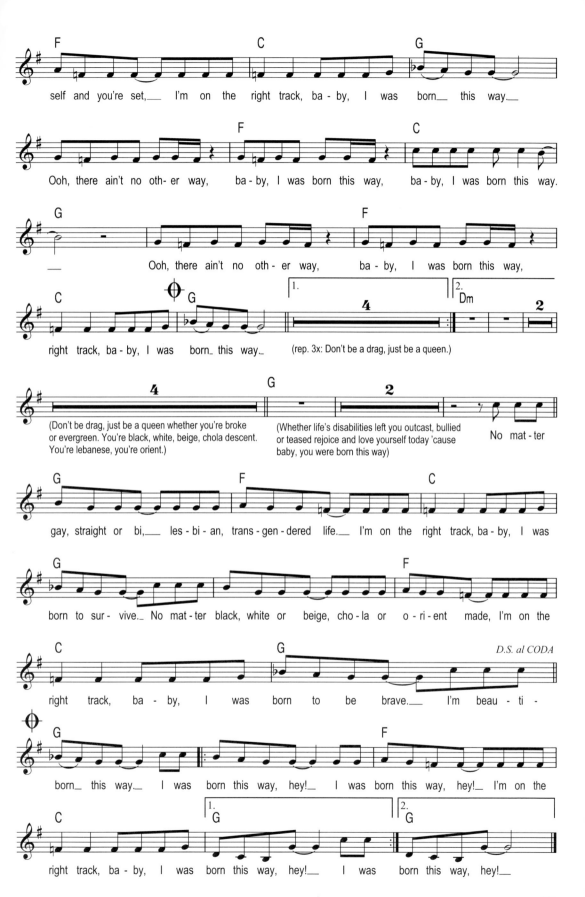

BROKEN STRINGS
JAMES MORRISON FEAT. NELLY FURTADO

♩ = 112   8-Beat

Leadsound: Flute

Musik & Text: Nina Woodford, James Morrison & Fraser Thorneycroft-Smith
© Copyright 2008 Chrysalis Music Limited. Alle Rechte für Deutschland, Österreich, Schweiz
GLOBAL MUSIKVERLAG, München / Sony/ATV Music Publishing (UK) Limited.
All Rights Reserved. International Copyright Secured.

34

CAN'T GET YOU OUT OF MY HEAD   KYLIE MINOGUE

♩ = 126	Disco-Beat
Leadsound: Vibraphone	

Musik & Text: Cathy Dennis & Rob Davis
© Copyright 2001 EMI Music Publishing Limited. Reproduced by permission of Faber Music Limited) / Universal/MCA Music Limited
(Administered in Germany by Universal/MCA Music Publishing GmbH).
All Rights Reserved. International Copyright Secured.

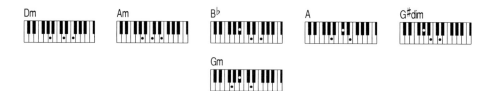

La la la la___ la la la la. La la la la___

___ la la la la. La la la la___ la la la la. La la la la___ la la I just

can't get you out of my head. Boy your lov-in' is all I think a-bout. I just

can't get you out of my head. Boy it's more than I dare to think a-bout.

Ev - 'ry night, e - ve - ry day just to___ be there in___ your arms.
There's a dark se - cret in me. Don't leave___ me locked in___ your heart.

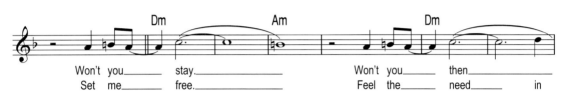

Won't you_____ stay._____ Won't you_____ then_____
Set me_____ free._____ Feel the_____ need_____ in

— stay_ for - ev - er___ and ev - er___ and ev - er___ and ev - er.___
me.

D.S. al CODA

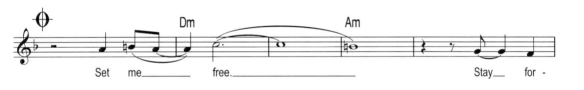

Set me_____ free._____ Stay___ for -

-ev - er___ and ev - er___ and ev - er___ and ev - er._____

rep. ad lib.

La la la la___ la la la la. La la la la___ la la la la.

CHASING CARS
SNOW PATROL

Musik & Text: Gary Lightbody, Nathan Connolly, Jonathan Quinn, Paul Wilson & Tom Simpson
© Copyright 2006 Universal Music Publishing BL Limited.
All rights in Germany administered by Universal Music Publishing GmbH.
All Rights Reserved. International Copyright Secured.

♩ = 104	8-Beat
Leadsound: Flute	

We'll do it all, ev-'ry-thing on our own.

We don't need an-y-thing or an-y-one.

If I lay here, if I just lay here would you lie with me and just for-get the world?

I don't quite know how to say how I feel.
Let's waste time cha-sing cars a-round our heads.

Those three words are
I need your grace to

said too much.   They're not e - nough.   If I lay
re - mind me,   to find my own.

here,   if I just lay here   would you lie with me and

just for - get the world?   For - get what we're told   be - fore we get

too old.   Show me a gar - den that's burst - ing in - to life.

All that I am,   all that I ev - er was

is here in your per - fect eyes, they're all I can see.

I don't know where   con - fused a - bout how as well

just know that these things will nev - er change for us at all.

If I lay here,   if I just lay here

would you lie with me and just for - get the world?

CHASING PAVEMENTS
ADELE

♩ = 80	8 Beat
	Leadsound: Oboe

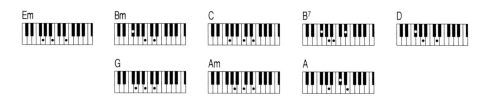

I've made up my mind. Don't need to think it o-ver if I'm

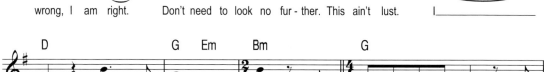

wrong, I am right. Don't need to look no fur-ther. This ain't lust. I

know this is love. But if I tell the world, I'll

nev-er say e-nough, cause it was not said to you. And that's ex-act-ly what I need to do if

I'm in love with you, should I give up or should I

just keep chas-ing pave-ments? E-ven if it leads no-where. Or

would it be a waste. E-ven if I knew my place, should I leave it there?

CLINT EASTWOOD
GORILLAZ

♩ = 84	8-Beat
	Leadsound: Harmonica

Musik & Text: Damon Albarn, Jamie Hewlett, Ed Case & Sweetie Irie
© 2001 Sony/ATV Music Publishing (UK) Limited / Sweets Music / EMI Music Publishing Limited, London.
Reproduced by permission of International Music Publications (a trading name of Faber Music Limited). All Rights Reserved.

Dm   G   C

I ain't

hap-py, I'm feel-ing glad._ I got sun-shine in a bag._ I'm use-less but

not for long,_ the fu-ture is com-ing on._ I ain't

1. com-ing on,_ is

2.

com-ing on,_ is com-ing on,_ is com-ing on,_ is com-ing on._

1.-3.

(Rap): Finally someone let me out of my cage. Now, time for me is nothing cos I'm counting no age. Now I couldn't be there, now you shouldn't be scared. I'm good at repairs and I'm under each snare. Intangible, bet you didn't think so I command you to panoramic view, look I'll make it all manageable. Pick and choose, sit and lose, all you different crews, chicks and dudes. Who you think is really kickin' tunes? Picture you gettin' down in a picture tube like you lit the fuse, you think it's fictional, mystical? Maybe spiritual, hearable. What appears in you is a clearer view cos you're too crazy. Lifeless to know the definition for what life is Priceless for you because I put you on the hype shit. You like it? Gunsmokin' righteous with one token. Psychic among those possess you with one go.

4.   Dm

I ain't hap-py, I'm feel-ing glad._ I got sun-shine in a bag._ I'm

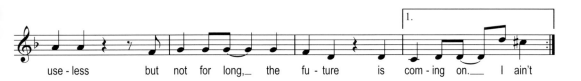

use - less   but   not   for   long,__   the   fu - ture   is   com - ing   on.__   I   ain't

com - ing   on,__   is   com - ing   on,__   is   com - ing   on,__   is   com - ing   on,__   is   com - ing   on.__

Dm   G   Dm   C

(Rap): The essence the basics without it you make it. Allow me to make this childlike in nature. Rhythm you have it or you don't, that's a fallacy. I'm in them every sprouting tree, every child apiece, every cloud you see, you see with your eyes. I see destruction and demise, corruption in disguise. From this fuckin' enterprise, now I'm sucking to your lies. Through Russ, though not his muscles but the percussion he provides.

Dm   1.

(Rap): With me as a guide but y'all can see me now cos you don't see with your eye. You perceive with your mind, that's the inner. So I'm gonna stick around with Russ and be a mentor, bust a few rhymes so mother fuckers remember where the thought is. I brought all this so you can survive when law is lawless. Feelings, sensations that you thought were dead, no squealing, remember that it's all in your head.

I   ain't   hap - py,   I'm   feel - ing   glad.__   I   got   sun - shine   in   a   bag.__   I'm

use - less   but   not   for   long,__   my   fu - ture   is   com - ing   on.__   I   ain't

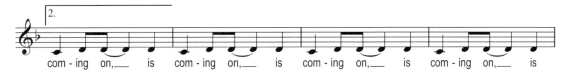

com - ing   on,__   is   com - ing   on,__   is   com - ing   on,__   is   com - ing   on,__   is

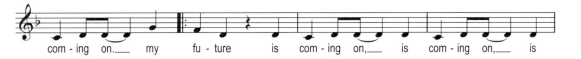

com - ing   on.__   my   fu - ture   is   com - ing   on,__   is   com - ing   on,__   is

rep. ad lib.

com - ing   on,__   is   com - ing   on,__   is   com - ing   on.__   my

COLD SHOULDER
ADELE

Musik & Text: Adele Adkins
© Copyright 2007 Universal Music Publishing Limited.
All rights in Germany administered by Universal Music Publishing GmbH.
All Rights Reserved. International Copyright Secured.

♩ = 110   8-Beat

Leadsound: Flute

You
say it's all in my head, and the things I think just don't make
sense. So where you been_ then? Don't go all coy. Don't turn it
round on_ me like it's my fault. See, I can see that look in
your eyes. The one that shoots on me each and ev-'ry time. You
grace me with your cold shoul-der.__ When-ev-er you look at me I wish I was
her.__ You show-er me with words made of knives. When-ev-er
you look at me I wish I was her.__

COME UNDONE
ROBBIE WILLIAMS

♩ = 84   8-Beat

Leadsound: Saxophone

Musik & Text: Robbie Williams, Boots Ottestad, Ashley Hamilton & Daniel Pierre
© 2002 Universal Music Publishing MGB Limited / EMI April Music Incorporated / EMI Blackwood Music Incorporated.
EMI Music Publishing Limited, London. Twenty Seven Songs/ Kobalt Music Publishing Limited.
Reproduced by permission of International Music Publications Limited (a trading name of Faber Music Limited).
All Rights Reserved.

So un-im-pressed but so in awe.
So rock and roll,__ so corp'-rate suit.

__ Such a saint__ but such a whore.
__ So damn ug-__ly, so damn cute.

So self a-ware, so__ full of__ shit.
So well trained, so__ a-ni-mal.

So in-de-ci-sive, so__ a-dam-ant
So need your love, so__ fuck you all.

__ I'm con-tem-pla-ting, think-ing a-bout__ think-ing. It's so frust-
__ I'm not scared of dy-ing I just don't want__ to. If I stopped

-ra-ting, just get a-no-ther drink__ in. Watch me come un-done.
ly-ing I'd just dis-ap-point__ you. I come un-done.

__ They're sell-ing ra-zor blades__ and mir-rors in__ the street.__

Pray__ that when I'm com-ing down__ you'll be a-sleep.__

If I ev-er hurt__ you your re-venge__ will be__ so sweet, be-cause I'm

47

COMPLICATED
AVRIL LAVIGNE

♩ = 78 | Rock Beat

Leadsound: Flute

Musik & Text: Lauren Christy, David Alspach, Graham Edwards and Avril Lavigne
© Copyright 2002 WB Music Corporation/Warner-Tamerlane Publishing Corporation / Almo Music Corporation /
Avril Lavigne Publishing Limited / Rainbow Fish Publishing / Mr. Spock Music / Ferry Hill Songs, USA.
Warner/Chappell North America Limited, London. Reproduced by permission of Faber Music Limited.
Rondor Music International (administered in Germany by Rondor Musikverlag GmbH).
All Rights Reserved. International Copyright Secured.

- ed? See, the way you're act-ing like you're some-bod-y else gets me frus-trat-

- ed. Life's like this, you, you fall___ and you crawl___ and you break and you take

___ what you get___ and you turn___ it in - to hon - es - ty.___ Pro - mise me I'm

1.

nev - er gon - na find ya fake___ it. No, no,_____ no.

2. *D.S. al CODA*

No, no.___ No, no, why'd you have to go and make things so com - pli - cat-

- ed? See, the way you're act - ing like you're some - bod - y else gets me frus - trat-

- ed. Life's like this, you, you fall___ and you crawl___ and you break and you take

___ what you get___ and you turn___ it in - to hon - es - ty.___ Pro - mise me I'm

nev - er gon - na find ya fake___ it. No, no,_____ no.___

49

DANCE WITH SOMEBODY
MANDO DIAO

♩ = 148	Disco Beat
Leadsound: Saxophone	

Musik & Text: Bjoern Dixgard, Gustaf Noren
© Universal Music Publishing GmbH (Germany).

Break your hap - py home,___
When you're all___ a - lone___

learn to sing a - long___ to the mu - sic, to the mu - sic.
we be - come your home.___ We're the mu - sic, we're the mu - sic.

Clap your hands and shake___ on a sum - mer's day___
When your love's_ a - way___ and you feel___ be - trayed

___ to the mu - sic, to the mu - sic.
___ we're the mu - sic, sweet mu - sic. I'm fall - ing in love

___ with your fav - 'rite song,_____ I'm go - nna sing___ it all___ night long,

_____ I'm gon - na dance_ with some - bod - y, dance_ with some - bod - y, dance,

dance, dance.___ I'm fall-ing in love_ with your fav-'rite song,___ I'm go-nna sing

___ it all___ night long,___ I'm gon-na dance_ with some-bod-y, dance

___ with some-bod-y, dance,___ dance, dance.___

I'm fall-ing in love___ with your fav-'rite song,___ I'm go-nna sing_

___ it all___ night long,___ I'm gon-na dance_ with some-bod-y, dance

rep. ad lib.

___ with some-bod-y, dance,___ dance, dance.___ I'm fall-ing in love_

51

DAS MODEL
KRAFTWERK

♩ = 123	8-Beat
Leadsound: Synth Lead	

Musik: Karl Bartos, Ralf Hütter / Text: Emil Schult, Ralf Hütter
© Copyright 1978 Kling Klang Musik GmbH / Edition Positive Songs, Hanseatic Musikverlag GmbH & Co KG.
Alle Rechte für Deutschland, Österreich, Schweiz bei Sony/ATV (Germany) GmbH und
Warner/Chappell Overseas Holdings Limited, London. Reproduced by permission of Faber Music Limited.
All Rights Reserved. International Copyright Secured.

Sie stellt sich zur Schau für das Kon - sum - pro - dukt.

Und wird von Mil - lio - nen Au - gen an - ge - guckt.

Ihr neu - es Ti - tel - bild ist ein - fach fa - bel - haft.

Ich muss sie wie - der - sehn, ich las, sie

hat's ge - schafft.

DON'T SPEAK
NO DOUBT

♩ = 76 Rock Beat

Leadsound: Flute

Musik & Text: Eric Stefani & Gwen Stefani

DON'T STOP THE DANCE
BRYAN FERRY

♩ = 130	8 Beat
	Leadsound: Saxophone

Ma-ma__ says truth is all that__ mat - ters.__ Ly - ing__ and de -

ceiv - ing is a sin. Drift - ing__ through a world__ torn and tat - tered.

Ev -'ry__ thought I have don't mean a thing.__ Don't stop,

don't stop the dance.__ Don't, (more mu - sic)__ don't stop the dance.

__ Ma - ma__ says love is all that__ mat - ters.__

Beau - ty__ should be dee - per than the skin. Liv - ing for the mo - ment,

DON'T LOOK BACK IN ANGER
OASIS

♩ = 82	Rock Beat
Leadsound: Piano	

Musik & Text: Noel Gallagher
© Copyright 1995 Creation Songs Limited / Oasis Music (GB).
Sony/ATV Music Publishing (UK) Limited.
All Rights Reserved. International Copyright Secured.

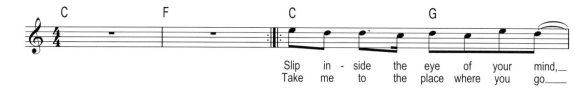

Slip in - side the eye of your mind,__
Take me to the place where you go__

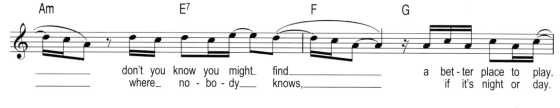

don't you know you might__ find__ a bet - ter place to play.
where__ no - bo - dy__ knows,__ if it's night or day.

You said that you'd ne - ver been__
Please don't put your life in the hands__

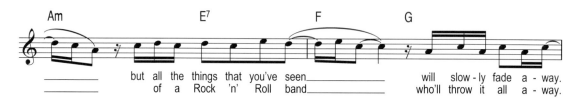

but all the things that you've seen__ will slow - ly fade a - way.
of a Rock 'n' Roll band__ who'll throw it all a - way.

So I start a re - vo - lu - tion from my bed 'cause you

said the brains I had went to my head. Step out - side__ the sum - mer - time's in

DU ERINNERST MICH AN LIEBE
ICH + ICH

♩ = 62 | 8 Beat

Leadsound: Oboe

Musik & Text: Annette Humpe
© by Ambulanz Musikverlag Annette Humpe.

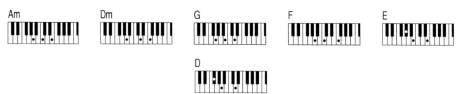

Wenn mei - ne See - le grau ist, nichts macht mehr Sinn.___ Ich bin ganz o - ben, und ich
Wo - zu der gan - ze Kampf um Macht und___ Geld? Was soll ich sam - meln hier auf

weiß nicht mehr, wo - hin ich gehn soll. Mmh._____
die - ser Welt, wenn ich doch gehn muss, wenn mein Tag ge - kom - men ist?

Wo vie - le Schat - ten sind, da ist auch Licht.___
Wenn mei - ne in - n're Stim - me zu mir spricht,___

Ich lau - fe zu dir, ich ver - gess dich nicht.___ Du kennst mich
ich bin taub und hör sie nicht,___ dann schau mich an

und mein wah - res Ge - sicht._____
und___ hal - te mich._____ Du er - in - nerst mich an

Lie - be, ich kann se - hen, wer du wirk - lich bist.___ Du er - in - nerst mich da-

60

61

G D.S. al CODA
ran, wie es sein kann.
Er - in - ner mich an
Am Dm
Lie - be, zeig mir, wer du wirk - lich bist._ Er - in - ner mich da-
G 1. 2. E Am
ran, wie es sein kann. Er - in - ner mich an Da ist ein Weg, so weit,
E G D Am E
_ und en - det in Un - end - lich - keit._ Da ist ein Fluss, lang und schön,_
G D F
ich kann das En - de nicht sehn, ich kann das En - de_ nicht
E Am F G
sehn.
Am
Du er - in - nerst mich an Lie - be, ich kann se - hen, wer du wirk - lich bist._
Dm G
Du er - in - nerst mich da - ran, wie es sein kann. Er - in - ner mich an
Am Dm
Lie - be, zeig mir, wer du wirk - lich bist._ Er - in - ner mich da-
G Am
ran, wie es sein kann. Wenn mei - ne See - le grau ist, nichts macht mehr Sinn.
F Dm E
Ich bin ganz o - ben, und ich weiß nicht mehr, wo - hin ich gehn soll. Mmh._

ELEKTRISCHES GEFÜHL
JULI

♩ = 176	Pop Beat
Leadsound: Synth Lead	

Musik: Simon Triebel / Text: Eva Briegel, Simon Triebel
© by EMI Music Publishing Germany GmbH.

Dm — Bb — F — C — Gm

A - tem - los und fern - ge - steu - ert,

ab - ge - stumpft und sor - gen - schwer. Ich bin völ - lig weg - ge - tre - ten, ich spür mich

selbst nicht mehr. Ich will aus fünf - zehn Me - tern ins kal - te Was - ser spring'n,

da - mit ich wie - der merk, dass ich am Le - ben bin. Ich geh nach vor - ne, bis
Al - les um mich he - rum

___ zum Rand, ich spür mein Herz pul - siern. Ich at - me ein und lass___
___ pul - siert,___ ich spür den Schmerz nicht mehr. Der Bo - den, die Wand, der Raum

___ mich fal - len, ich spü - re je - den Teil von mir. E - lek - tri - sches Ge - fühl,
___ vib - riert___ ich bin___ wie - der un - besch - wert. E - lek - tri - sches Ge - fühl

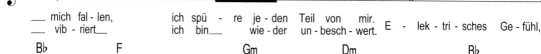

___ ich bin völ - lig___ schwe - re - los. E - lek - tri - sches Ge - fühl,___

62

wie beim ers-ten A-tem-zug. E-lek-tri-sches Ge-fühl,___ und die Stim-me,___

dir mir sagt, heu-te wird ein gu-ter Tag, heu-te wird_ ein gu-ter_ Tag.

Auch wenn mich tau-send Sor-gen quä-len und sie mich nach un-ten ziehn.

Es ist bes-ser los-zu-las-sen, als dran ka-putt zu gehn.

Ich neh-me, was mir Angst macht, und ich schreib es auf Pa-pier.

D.S. al CODA 1

Ich zünd es an und lass es bren-nen,___ ich_ lass es hin-ter mir.

3x

Oh, oh, oh. Oh, oh. Oh, oh, oh. Oh, oh, oh.

Al-les was dich run-ter zieht, al-les was dein Herz lahm legt,
Al-les was nicht wich-tig ist, a-les was nicht rich-tig ist,

D.S. al CODA 2

lass es los. Lass es los. Lass es los. E-

rep. ad lib.

Heu-te wird_ ein gu-ter_ Tag.

63

FIREWORK
KATY PERRY

♩ = 124 | 8 Beat

Leadsound: Flute

Musik & Text: Katy Perry, Mikkel Storleer Eriksen, Tor Erik Hermansen, Sandy Julien Wilhelm & Ester Dean
© 2010 When I'm Rich You'll Be My Bitch administered by W B Music Corporation, EMI Music Publishing Limited, Ultra Tunes and
Peermusic III Limited / 2412 LLC Dat Damn Dean Music. EMI Music Publishing Limited, London and Warner/Chappell North
America Limited, London. Reproduced by permission of International Music Publications Limited (a trading name of Faber
Music Limited) and Faber Music Limited/ Für Deutschland: Peermusic (Germany) GmbH. All Rights Reserved.

_____ like the fourth___ of___ Ju - ly.____ Cause ba - by you're a

fi - re - work.___ Come on show 'em what you're worth.___ Make 'em go "Oh, oh,___ oh!"

As you shoot a - cross the sky - y - y. Ba - by you're a fi - re - work.

___ Come on let your co - lors burst.___ Make 'em go "Oh, oh,___ oh!"

You're gon - na leave 'em fal - lin' down - own - own._____

Boom, boom,___ boom. E - ven brigh - ter than the moon, moon,___ moon.

It's al - ways been in - side of you,____ you,____ you.

And now it's time to let it through._____ Cause ba - by you're a

Boom, boom, boom. E - ven brigh - ter than the moon, moon, moon.

65

FIRST DAY OF MY LIFE
MELANIE C.

♩ = 78	8-Beat
Leadsound: Piano	

Musik & Text: Enrique Iglesias, Guy Chambers

1. So I found a rea - son___ to stay a - live.
   rea - son___ to let it go.

Try a lit - tle har - der___ see the oth - er side.__ Talk - ing to my - self
Tell you that I'm smil - ing___ but I still need to grow. Will I find sal - va -

___ too man - y sleep - less nights. Tryin' to find a mean - ing_ to this stu - pid life.
tion in the arms of love. Will it stop me search - ing,__ will it be e - nough.

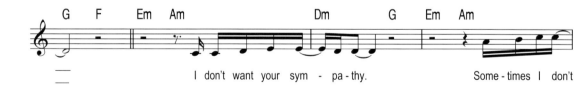

___ I don't want your sym - pa - thy. Some - times I don't

_ know who to be.___ Hey, what you're look - ing for,___ no one has the

FRIDAY I'M IN LOVE
THE CURE

♩ = 136 | Pop Beat

Leadsound: Saxophone

Text: Robert Smith / Musik: Robert Smith, Simon Gallup, Porl Thompson, Boris Williams & Perry Bamonte
© Copyright 1992 Fiction Songs Limited.
All Rights Reserved. International Copyright Secured.

- day, I'm in love.__ Sa - tur - day__ wait,__ Sun - day al - ways comes

__ too late. Fri - day, nev - er he - si - tate. Dressed up to the eyes,

__ it's a won - der - ful sur - prise__ to see your shoes__ and your spi - rits rise.__

__ Throw - ing out your frown__ and just smil - ing at the sound,__ as sleek as a sheik

__ spinn - ing round and round.__ Al - ways take a big bite,__ it's such a gor - geous sight

__ to see you eat__ in the mid - dle of the night.__ You can nev - er get e - nough,

__ e - nough of this stuff. It's Fri - day, I'm__ in love.__

I don't care if Mon - day's blue, Tues - day's grey and Wednes - day too.__

Thurs - day I don't care__ a - bout you.__ It's Fri - day, I'm in love.__

__ Mon - day you can fall__ a - part, Tues - day, Wednes - day break

__ my heart. Thurs - day does - n't e - ven start. It's Fri - day I'm in love.

__

GEBOREN UM ZU LEBEN
UNHEILIG

♩ = 92 | Rock Beat

Leadsound: Piano

Musik: Henning Verlage, Der Graf / Text: Der Graf
© Fansation M.Tombuelt & O. Reimann GbR / Universal Music Publishing GmbH/ Copyright Control.

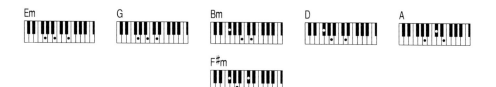

Es fällt mir schwer, oh - ne dich zu le - ben,_ je - den Tag zu je - der Zeit,_ ein - fach al - les zu ge - ben. Ich denk so oft__ zu - rück an das, was war,_ an je - dem so ge - lieb - ten ver - gan - ge - nen__ Tag.__ Ich stell mir vor, dass du zu mir stehst, und je - den mei - ner We - ge an mei - ner Sei - te gehst. Ich den - ke an__ so vie - les, seit - dem du nicht mehr bist,__ denn du hast mir ge - zeigt,__ wie wert - voll das Le - ben ist.

Bm   D

Wir warn ge-bo-ren um__ zu le - ben,__ mit den Wun-dern je-ner Zeit.

A   Em

__ Sich nie-mals zu ver-ges - sen,__ bis in al-le E - wig-keit.

G   Bm

_ Wir warn ge-bo-ren um__ zu le - ben,__ für den ei-nen Au-gen-blick,

A   G   F#m   Em

_ bei dem je-der von uns spür - te__ wie wert-voll Le-ben__ ist.

       G   Bm

Es tut noch weh, wie-der Neu-em Platz zu schaf-fen. Mit gu-tem Ge-fühl,__ et-was

D   Em   G

Neu-es zu-zu-las-sen. In die-sem Au-gen-blick, bist du mir wie-der nah,__ wie an

Bm   D   Em

je-dem so ge-lieb-ten ver-gan-ge-nen Tag__ Es ist mein Wunsch, wie-der

G   Bm

Träu-me zu er-lau - ben,__ oh-ne Reu-e nach vorn__ in ei-ne

D   Em   G

Zu-kunft zu schaun. Ich se-he ei-nen Sinn, seit-dem du nicht mehr bist.__ Denn

du hast mir ge - zeigt,___ wie wert - voll mein Le - ben ist.

Wir warn ge - bo - ren um___ zu le - ben,___ mit den Wun - dern je - ner Zeit.

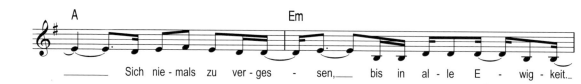
_____ Sich nie - mals zu ver - ges - sen,___ bis in al - le E - wig - keit.

_ Wir warn ge - bo - ren um___ zu le - ben,___ für den ei - nen Au - gen - blick,

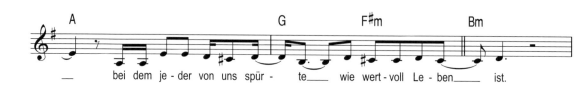
_ bei dem je - der von uns spür - te___ wie wert - voll Le - ben___ ist.

Wie wert - voll Le - ben___ ist. Wir warn ge - bo - ren um___ zu

le - ben,___ mit den Wun - dern je - ner___ Zeit. Ge - bo - ren um___ zu le - ben.

Wir warn ge-bo-ren um__ zu le - ben,__ mit den Wun-dern je-ner Zeit.

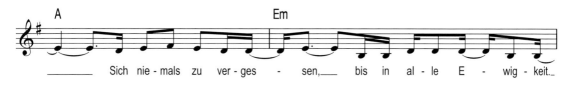
____ Sich nie-mals zu ver-ges - sen,__ bis in al-le E - wig-keit.__

__ Wir warn ge-bo-ren um__ zu le - ben,__ für den ei-nen Au-gen-blick,

__ bei dem je-der von uns spür - te__ wie wert-voll Le - ben

1.
ist. Wir warn ge-bo-ren um__ zu le -
2.
ist.

Wir warn ge-bo-ren um__ zu le - ben.__

repeat ad lib. and fade out

GIB MIR SONNE
ROSENSTOLZ

♩ = 71 | 8 Beat

Leadsound: Piano

Musik & Text: Peter Plate, Ulf Leo Sommer, AnNa R.
© Partitur Musikverlag / Arabella Musikverlag GmbH (Universal Music Publ. Group).

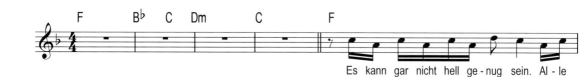

Es kann gar nicht hell ge - nug sein. Al - le

Lich - ter die - ser Welt___ sol - len heu - te für mich leuch - ten. Ich werd raus - gehn, mich nicht

um - drehn, ich muss weg.

Manch - mal muss Lie - be schnell gehn,___ mich ü - ber -
Und ich tra - ge mein Herz of - fen,___ al - le

fahrn, mich ü - ber - rolln.___ Manch - mal muss das Le - ben
Tü - ren ganz weit auf.___ Hab kei - ne Angst, mich zu ver -

weh tun, nur wenn's weh tut, ist es gut, da - für zu gehn.
bren - nen. Auch wenn's weh tut, nur was weh tut, ist auch gut.___

___ Gib mit Son - ne,___ gib mir Wär - me, gib mir Licht, all die Far - ben wie - der zu - rück.
___

Ver - brenn den Schnee, das Grau muss weg. Schenk mir ein biss - chen Glück. Wann kommt die Son - ne? Kann es denn sein, dass mir gar nichts mehr ge - lingt? Wann kommt die Son - ne? Kannst du nicht sehn, dass ich tief im Schnee ver - sink.

Fei - er das Le - ben, fei - er das Glück. Fei - er uns bei - de, es kommt al - les zu - rück. Fei - er die Lie - be, fei - er den Tag. Fei - er uns bei - de, es ist al - les ge - sagt. Hier kommt die Son - ne, hier kommt das Licht. Siehst du, die Far - ben komm' al - le zu - rück.

Hier kommt die Son - ne.

Hier kommt die Son - ne.

GO LET IT OUT
OASIS

♩ = 85	Rock Beat
	Leadsound: Saxophone

Musik & Text: Noel Gallagher

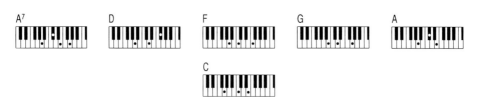

Paint no il - lu - sion, try to click with what - cha got.___

Taste ev - 'ry por - tion_'cause if you like your - self_ a lot. Go let it out,___ go let it in,_

___ go let it out.___ Life is pre - co - cious in a

most pe - cu - liar way. Sis - ter psy - cho - sis___ don't got a lot_ to say. She go let it out,

___ she go let it in,___ she go let it out.___ She go let it out,

Is it an - y won - der why prin - ces and kings_ are clowns that ca - per in their

saw - dust rings.___ Or - di - na - ry peo - ple that are like you and me,___ we're the

kee - pers of their des - ti - ny.___ We're the kee - pers of their des - ti - ny.___

I'm go - ing leav - ing this ci - ty, I'm go - ing driv - ing out - ta town. And

you're com - ing with___ me___ the right time is al - ways now.___ To go let it out,___

___ to go let it in,___ to go let it out.___ To go let it out,

Is it an - y won - der why prin - ces and kings___

are clowns that ca - per in their saw - dust rings.___ Or - di - na - ry peo - ple that are

like you and me,___ we're the kee - pers of their des - ti - ny.___ We're the

buil - ders of their des - ti - ny___ So go let it out,___

___ go let it in.___ Go let it out,___ don't let it in,

don't let it in, don't let it in.___

GOODBYE MY LOVER
JAMES BLUNT

♩ = 96	Ballad
Leadsound: Piano	

I've been ad-dic-ted to___ you.
I can-not live with-out___ you.
Good-bye___ my lo-ver. Good-bye___ my friend.

You have been the one. You have been the one for me. Good-bye___ my lo-ver.

Good-bye___ my friend.___ You have been the one. You have been the one for me.

I am a drea-mer but when I wake, you can't break my spi-rit,

it's my dreams you take. And as___ you move___ on, re-mem-ber me,

re-mem-ber us and all___ we used to be.___ I've

And I still___ hold your hand___ in mine,___ in mine___ when I'm a-sleep.

D.S. al CODA

And I will___ bear my soul___ in time,___ when I'm kneel-ing at your feet.___

I'm so hol-low, ba-by, I'm so hol-low. I'm so, I'm so,

I'm so hol-low.

79

HAUS AM SEE
PETER FOX

♩ = 123 | 8 Beat

Leadsound: Vibraphone

Musik: David Conen, Pierre Baigorry, Vincent Graf Schlippenbach, Ruth-Maria Renner / Text: David Conen, Pierre Baigorry
© 2008 fixx & foxy Publishing / Soular Music GmbH & Co KG, Hanseatic Musikverlag GmbH & Co KG/
Warner/Chappell Overseas Holdings Limited. Reproduced by permission of Faber Music Limited.
All Rights Reserved.

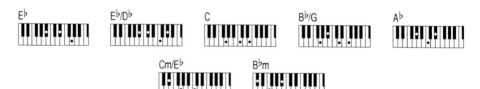

Huh, huh, eeh yeah.___ Huh, huh, eeh yeah.___
(Chor 1. x tacet)

Hier bin ich ge- born und lau- fe durch die Stra- ßen. Kenn die Ge- sich- ter, je- des

Haus und je- den La- den. Ich muss mal weg, kenn je- de Tau- be hier beim Na- men. Dau- men

raus, ich war- te auf 'ne schi- cke Frau mit schnel- lem Wa- gen.

Die Son- ne blen- det, al- les fliegt vor- bei. Und die Welt hin- ter mir wird

lang- sam__ klein.__ Doch__ die Welt vor mir ist für mich ge- macht.

Ich weiß sie war - tet und ich hol sie ab. Ich hab den Tag auf mei - ner Sei - te, ich hab

Rü - cken - wind. Ein Frau - en - chor am Stra - ßen - rand, der für mich singt. Ich

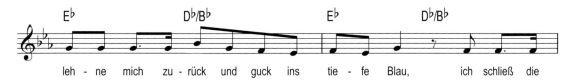

leh - ne mich zu - rück und guck ins tie - fe Blau, ich schließ die

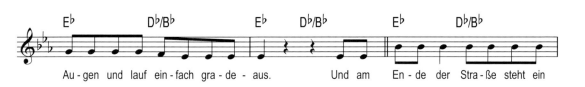

Au - gen und lauf ein - fach gra - de - aus. Und am En - de der Stra - ße steht ein

Haus am__ See.__ O - ran - gen - baum - blät - ter lie - gen auf dem__ Weg.__ Ich

hab zwan - zig Kin - der, mei - ne Frau ist__ schön. Al - le komm'n vor - bei, ich brauch nie

raus - zu - gehn. (Im Traum ge - sehn,__ das Haus am See.)__

Huh, huh eeh yeah.__ Huh, huh eeh yeah.. Ich

su-che neu-es Land mit un-be-kann-ten Stra-ßen, frem-de Ge-sich-ter und

kei-ner kennt mein' Na-men! Al-les ge-win-nen beim Spiel mit ge-zink-ten Kar-ten. Al-

-les ver-liern, Gott hat ei-nen har-ten lin-ken Ha-ken. Ich gra-be Schät-ze aus im

Schnee und Sand, und Frau-en rau-ben mir je-den Ver-stand.

Doch ir-gend-wann werd ich vom Glück ver-folgt und komm zu-rück mit bei-den

Ta-schen voll Gold. Ich lad die al-ten Vö-gel und Ver-wand-ten ein.

Und al-le fang'n vor Freu-de an zu wein'n. Wir grill'n, die Ma-mas ko-chen und wir

sau-fen Schnaps. Und fei-ern ei-ne Wo-che je-de Nacht. Und der

Mond scheint hell auf mein Haus am__ See,__ O-ran-gen-baum-blät-ter lie-gen

auf dem__ Weg.__ Ich hab zwan-zig Kin-der, mei-ne Frau ist__ schön.

83

HEAVY CROSS
GOSSIP

♩ = 120 | Rock Beat

Leadsound: E-Guitar

Musik & Text: Mary Beth Patterson, Nathan Howdeshell & Hannah Billie
© Chrysalis Music Limited. Alle Rechte für Deutschland, Österreich, Schweiz GLOBAL MUSIKVERLAG, München.

Em

D

Dm

Uh, uh,___ uh. Uh,___ uh.

___ Uh, uh,___ ___ It's a cruel cruel world, to face on your own.___ A

heav - y cross, to car - ry a - lone.___ The lights are on, but

eve - ry - one's gone and it's cruel.___ It's a fun - ny way,___ to

make ends meet,___ when the lights are out___ on eve - ry street.___ It

feels al - right,___ but nev - er com - plete, with - out___ you.___ I checked

you,_____ if it's al-read-y been done, un-do it. It takes

two,_ it's up to me and you, to prove_ it. All the rain-

-y nights,____ e-ven the cold-est days,_ you're mo-ments a-go,____ but

sec-onds a-way._ The prin-ci-pal_ of Nitz-sche, it's true but,_ it's a cruel

_ world._____ Uh,_ uh, uh.____ Uh,_ uh, uh.____ Uh,_ uh, uh._

_ Oh-uh-oh.___ We can play it safe,_____ or play it cool._

Fol-low the lead-er, or make up all the rules.___ What-ev-er you_ want, the

85

HERE WITHOUT YOU
3 DOORS DOWN

♩ = 70 8 Beat

Leadsound: Saxophone

Musik & Text: Brad Arnold, Matt Roberts & Todd Harrell
© Copyright 2002 Universal Music Publishing Limited.
All rights in Germany administered by Universal Music Publ. GmbH.
All Rights Reserved. International Copyright Secured.

Am

F

G

C

A hun-dred days have made me old-

-er___ since the last___ time that I saw___ your pret-ty face.

A thou-sand lies have made me cold-er___ and I don't___ think I can look

___ at this___ the same.___ But all the miles

_ that sep-a-rate,___ they dis-ap-pear___ now when I'm___

dream-ing of your face.___ I'm here with-out___ you ba - by,___

but you're still on___ my lone-ly mind. I think a-bout___ you ba - by

HELLO (TURN YOUR RADIO ON)
QUEENSBERRY

♩ = 60 | 8 Beat

Leadsound: Synth Lead

Musik & Text: Marcella Detroit, Siobhan Fahey, Jean Guiot, Marcy Levy

Woke up this morn-ing and_ the
Woke up this morn-ing and_ my

streets were full of cars, all bright and shin-y like they'd just ar-rived from Mars.
head was in a daze, a brave new world has dawned up-on the hu-man race.

And as I stumb-led through last nights drun-ken de-bris
Where words are mean-ing less and ev'-ry-thing's sur-real.

the pa-per-boy_ screamed out the head-lines in the street.
I'm gon-na have to reach_ my friends to find out how I feel.

A-noth-er war and now the pound is look-ing weak and tell me have you read_ a-
And if I taste the ho-ney is it real-ly sweet, and do I eat it with_ my

-bout the la-test freak? We're bin-go num-bers and our names are ob-so-lete
hands or with my feet? Does a-ny-bo-dy real-ly lis-ten when I speak

why do I feel bit-ter when_ I should be feel-ing sweet.   Hel-lo,_
or will I have to say_ it all a-gain next week?

91

HOT 'N' COLD
KATY PERRY

♩ = 132	Disco Beat
Leadsound: Flute	

Musik & Text: Lukasz Gottwald, Max Martin and Katy Perry
© 2007 Copyright 2008 Kasz Money Publishing/Maratone, AB/When I'm Rich You'll Be My Bitch, USA.
Kobalt Music Publishing Limited/ Warner/Chappell North America Limited.
Reproduced by permission of Faber Music Limited.
All Rights Reserved. International Copyright Secured.

You change your mind___ like a girl___ chan-ges clothes.

___ Yeah, you P M S___ like a bitch___ I would know.

___ And you o-ver-think___ al-ways speak___ cryp-ti-cally.

___ I should know___ that you're___ no good_ for me.___

___ Cause you're hot___ then you're cold, you're yes___ then you're no. You're in___

and you're out, you're up___ and you're down. You're wrong___ when it's right, it's black

___ and it's white. We fight,___ we break up, we kiss,___ we make up.

You, you don't real-ly want to stay no.___ You,___ should you real-ly want to

go, oh.___ You're hot___ then you're cold, you're yes___ then you're no. You're in___

___ and you're out, you're up___ and you're down.

Fine

93

HUMAN
THE KILLERS

J = 136 | 8 Beat

Leadsound: Synth Lead

Musik & Text: Brandon Flowers, Dave Keuning, Mark Stoermer & Ronnie Vannucci
© Copyright 2008 Universal Music Publishing Limited.
All rights in Germany administered by Universal Music Publishing GmbH.
All Rights Reserved. International Copyright Secured.

1. I did my best to no-tice, when the call came down the line.___ Up to the plat-form of sur-ren-der I was brought but I was kind.___ And some-times I get ner-vous, when I see an o-pen door.___ Close your eyes,___ clear your heart,___ cut the cord.___ Are we hu-man, or are we dan-cer. My sign is vi-tal, my hands are cold.__ And I'm on my knees,__ look-ing for the ans-wer. Are we hu-man, or are we dan-cer.

pects to grace and vir-tue, send my con-do-len-ces to good.___ Give my re-gards to soul and ro-mance, they al-ways did the best they could.___ And so long to de-vo-tion, you taught me e-ve-ry-thing I know. Wave good bye,___ wish me well,___ you've got-ta let me go.___

2. Pay my res-

94

I CRIED FOR YOU
KATIE MELUA

♩ = 62	Ballad
Leadsound: Piano	

Musik & Text: Katie Melua
© Copyright 2005 Melua Music Limited.
Sony/ATV Music Publishing (UK) Limited.
All Rights Reserved. International Copyright Secured.

G   F   C   D   Am

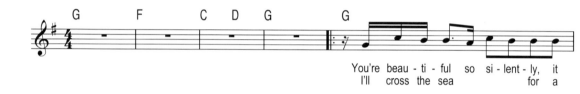

You're beau - ti - ful so si - lent - ly, it
I'll cross the sea for a

lies be - neath a shade of blue._ It struck me so vio - lent - ly when I looked at you.
diff' - rent world, with_ your trea - sure, a se - cret for me to____ hold.

But oth - ers pass, they nev - er pause, to feel that ma - gic in your hand._ To
In ma - ny years they may for - get this love of ours or that we met,_ they

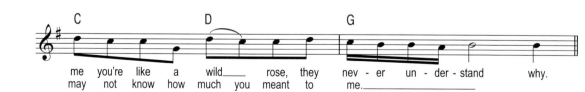

me you're like a wild____ rose, they nev - er un - der - stand why.
may not know how much you meant to me.____

96

I cried for you__ when the sky cried for you__ and when you went I be-came a hope-less drif-ter.__ But this life was not__ for you__ though I learned from you,__ that beau-ty need on-ly be a whis-per.

With-out you now I see how fra-gile__ the world can be. And I know you've gone a-way__ but in my heart__ you'll al-ways stay.__

D.S. al CODA

That beau-ty need on-ly be a whis-per.

I DON'T BELIEVE YOU
PINK

♩ = 92	Ballad
	Leadsound: Strings

Musik & Text: Alecia Moore, Max Martin
© Pink Inside Publishing / EMI Blackwood Music Inc.
Rechte für Deutschland, Österreich, Schweiz und Osteuropa (außer Baltikum): EMI Music Publishing Germany GmbH /
Kobalt Music Publishing Limited.

G   Em   Bm   C   D

Am

I don't mind it,_____ I don't mind at all.____
I don't mind it,_____ still don't mind at all.____

It's__ like you're the swing set,_____ and I'm the kid that falls.____
It's__ like one of those bad dreams,___ when you can't wake up.____

It's__ like the way_ we fight,___ the times I've cried.____ We come to blows,
It looks like, you've gi - ven up,___ you've had_ e - nough.___ But I__ want more,

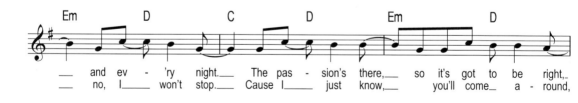

__ and ev - 'ry night.___ The pas - sion's there,___ so it's got to be right,
__ no, I__ won't stop.___ Cause I__ just know,___ you'll come_ a - round,

__ right?___ No,__ I don't be - lieve__ you,__ when you say__ don't
__ right?___

98

I NEED A DOLLAR
ALOE BLACC

♩ = 96	8 Beat
	Leadsound: Saxophone

Musik & Text: Aloe Blacc, Leon Michels, Nicholas Movshon & Jeffrey Silverman
© Copyright 2010 Kobalt Music Publishing Limited (75%) / Copyright Control (25%).
All Rights Reserved. International Copyright Secured.

I need a dol - lar, dol - lar, dol - lar is what I need.

Well I need a dol - lar, dol - lar, dol - lar is what I need. I need a dol - lar, dol - lar,

dol - lar is what I need._ And if I share with you_ my sto - ry would you

share your dol - lar with me._ Bad_ times are com - ing and I

reap what I don't sow._ Well let me tell_ you some - thing all that glit - ters ain't gold.

It's been a long_ old trou - ble long old trou - ble - some road._ And I'm

look - ing for_ some - bod - y come and help me car - ry this load._

I need a dol-lar, dol-lar, dol-lar is what I need. Well I need a dol-lar, dol-lar,

dol-lar is what I need. Well I don't know_ if I'm walk-ing on so-lid ground.

Cause ev - 'ry-thing a-round me_ is fall-ing down. And all I want is some

- one to help me._ I had a job_ but the boss man let me go._ He said:

I'm sor - ry but I won't be need-ing your help no more._ I said:

please_ mis - ter boss man I need this job more than you know._ But he

gave me my_ last pay-check and he sent me on out the door._

I need a dol-lar, dol-lar, dol-lar is what I need. Well I need a dol-lar, dol-lar,

dol-lar is what I need. I need a dol-lar, dol-lar, dol-lar is what I need. And if I

share with you___ my sto-ry would you share your dol-lar with me.___

Well I don't know___ if I'm walk-ing on so-lid ground.

Cause ev-'ry-thing a-round me___ is fall-ing down. And all I want is some

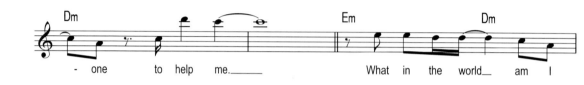

- one to help me._____ What in the world__ am I

gon-na do__ to-mor-row.___ Is there some-one with a dol-lar I__ could bor-row.

Who can help me take a-way my sor-row. May-be it's in - side the bot-tle.

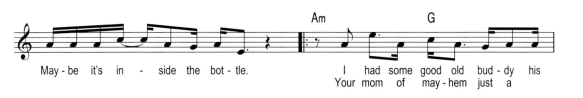

May-be it's in - side the bot-tle.

Am   G

I had some good old bud-dy his
Your mom of may-hem just a

Dm   Am   G

name is whis-key and wine.___ And for my good old bud-dy
child has got his own.___ If God has plans for me I hope

Dm   Am   G

I spent my last dime.___ My wine is good to me___ it
it ain't writ-ten in stone.___ Cause I've been work-ing work-ing my-

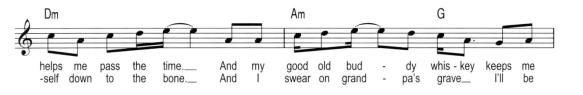

Dm   Am   G

helps me pass the time.___ And my good old bud - dy whis-key keeps me
-self down to the bone.___ And I swear on grand - pa's grave___ I'll be

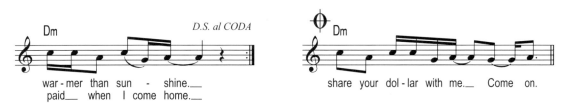

Dm   *D.S. al CODA*   Dm

war-mer than sun - shine.___   share your dol-lar with me.___ Come on.
paid___ when I come home.___

Am   G   Dm   *rep. ad lib.*

Share your dol-lar with me.___ Go___ a-head. Share your dol-lar with me.___ Come_ on.

I WILL LOVE YOU MONDAY
AURA DIONE

♩= 116 | Disco Beat

Leadsound: Synth Lead

Musik & Text: David Karl Aastroem, Kenneth Lungaard Bager, Patrik Jan Berggren, Aura Marie Dione, Per Ebdrup, Viktoria Magdalena Sandstroem
© Good Songs Publishing / Universal Music Publ. GmbH (Germany) / Kobalt Music Publishing Limited / Lifted Music/Reverb Music:
für D/A/CH: Musikverlag Progressive GmbH / EMI Music Publishing Germany GmbH.

Dum di du de dum_ da, dum dum di di du de dum_ ah. Dum di du de dum_ da,

dum dum di di du de dum. I will love you Mon - day_ and you will hurt me Tues - day_ And

I will kill you Thurs - day___ if you don't stop me Wednes - day.___ For -

give you on a Fri - day,_ re - un - ion on a Sa - tur - day,_ for - got - ten all on Sun - day,
so I can love you Mon - day

Three - hun - dred - six - ty - five___ days of the year

runn - ing round, runn - ing round, and go - ing no - where. Three - hun - dred - six - ty - five_

days and nights, three - hun - dred - six - ty - five_ tries to make it right._

Dum di du de dum_ da, dum dum di di du de dum_ ah. Dum di du de dum_ da,

Cm
D.S. al CODA 1

dum dum di di du de dum ah. Dum di du de dum_ da, dum dum di di du de dum.

Cm

I will love you Mon-day_ and you will hurt me Tues-day_ And I will kill you Thurs-day_ if

Fm

you don't stop me Wednes-day.___ For-give you on a Fri - day,___ re -

Cm

-un-ion on a Sa-tur-day,___ for-got-ten all on Sun-day___

Cm   Eb   Bb

Three-hun-dred-six-ty-five_ days of the year_ runn-ing round, runn-ing round, and

Ab   Eb   Bb   Cm

go-ing no-where. Three-hun-dred-six-ty-five_ days and nights,

Ab   Eb   Bb   Ab

three-hun-dred-six-ty-five_ tries to make it right._ Tries to make it right.

Cm

I will love you Mon-day_ and you will hurt me Tues-day_ I will love you Mon-day_ and

Fm

I will kill you Thurs-day_ For-give you on a Fri - day, yeah,_ yeah, yeah, yeah, yeah.

D.S.S. al CODA 2   Cm

_ Fri - day.___ Dum di du de dum_ da dum dum di di du de dum.

105

I'M OUTTA LOVE
ANASTACIA

♩ = 120	Rock Beat
Leadsound: Flute	

Musik & Text: Anastacia, Sam Watters & Louis Biancaniello
© Copyright 2000 Breakthrough Creations/ S.M.Y. Publishing / Sony/ATV Tunes LLC / PohoProductions, USA.
Sony/ATV Music Publishing (UK) Limited / Universal Music Publishing Limited. All rights in Germany administered by
Universal Music Publishing GmbH. All Rights Reserved. International Copyright Secured.

Now ba - by come on,___ don't claim___ that love you nev - er let me fear.
Said how ma - ny times___ have___ I tried to turn___ this love a - round?

___ I should have known_____ that you___ brought noth - ing real.
___ But ev - 'ry time_____ you___ just let___ me down.

___ Come on, be a man___ a - bout it, you___ won't die.___ I___
___ Come on, be a man___ a - bout it, you'll___ sur - vive,___ true.

___ ain't got no more tears___ to cry.___ And I can't___ take this no more,
___ that you can work it out___ al - right. Tell me yes - ter - day did you know

___ you know I got - ta let it go,___ and you know.___ I'm out - ta love,
___ I'd be the one to let you go,___ and you know.___

___ set___ me free___ and let me out___ this mi - se - ry.___ Just show me the way

___ to get___ my life a - gain_ 'cause you___ can't hand - le me.___ Said I'm out - ta love,

IN MY PLACE
COLDPLAY

♩ = 72	8 Beat
Leadsound: Piano	

Musik & Text: Guy Berryman, Chris Martin, Jon Buckland & Will Champion
© Copyright 2002 Universal Music Publishing MGB Limited.
All Rights in Germany Administered by Musik Edition Discoton GmbH (A Division of Universal Music Publishing Group).
All Rights Reserved. International Copyright Secured.

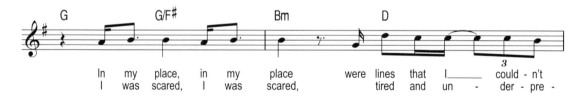

In my place, in my place were lines that I_____ could - n't
I was scared, I was scared, tired and un - der - pre -

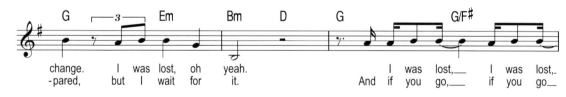

change. I was lost, oh yeah. I was lost,___ I was lost,___
-pared, but I wait for it. And if you go,___ if you go___

___ crossed lines I shoul - dn't have crossed. I was lost, oh yeah.
___ and leave me down here on my own, then I'll wait for you.

Yeah,___ how long must you wait for_____ it? Yeah, how long must you pay for___ ___ it? Yeah, how long must you wait for_____ it? Ah, for it?

Sing it please, please, please___ come back and sing to me, to me,___ me.___ Come on and sing it out, now, now___ come on and sing it out, to me,___ me,_____ come back and sing.___

In my place, in my place were lines that I could-n't change and I was lost, oh yeah.___ Oh_____ yeah.

109

IN THE SHADOWS
THE RASMUS

♩ = 106	Rock Beat
Leadsound: Organ	

Musik & Text: Lauri Ylonen, Eero Heinonen, Aki Hakala & Pauli Rantasalmi

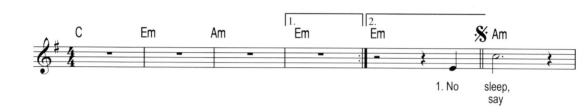

1. No sleep,
say

no sleep un - til I'm done with find - ing the ans - wer.__ Won't stop,
that I must learn to kill be - fore_ I can feel_ safe._ But I,

won't stop be - fore I find a cure_ for this can - cer.__ Some - times
I ra - ther kill my - self then turn_ in - to their_ slave. Some - times

I feel like go - ing down, I'm so_ dis - con - nec - ted._ Some - how_____
I feel that I should go and play_ with the thun - der._ Some - how_____

I know that I am haun - ted to be__ wan - ted._ I've been watch -
I just don't wan - na stay and wait for a won - der.

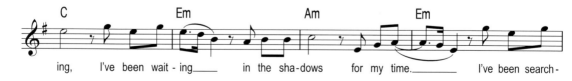

ing, I've been wait - ing_____ in the sha - dows for my time._____ I've been search -

IRGENDWAS BLEIBT
SILBERMOND

♩ = 100 | 8 Beat

Leadsound: Flute

Musik & Text: Stefanie Kloss, Andreas Jan Nowak, Johannes Stolle, Thomas Stolle
© EMI Songs Musikverlag GmbH/ Valicon Songs oHG adm. by EMI Songs Musikverlag GmbH / Silbermond Musikverlag GmbH/
Arabella Musikverlag GmbH (Universal Music Publishing Group).

Sag mir, dass die-ser Ort hier si-cher ist und al-les Gu-te steht hier still.___ Und dass das Wort, das du mir heu-te gibst, mor-gen noch ge-nau-so gilt. Die-se Welt ist schnell und hat ver-lernt, be-stän-dig zu sein.___ Denn Ver-su-chun-gen set-zen ih-re Frist.___ Doch bit-te schwör, dass, wenn ich wie-der komm, al-les noch beim Al-ten___ ist.___ Gib mir ein klei-nes biss-chen Si-cher-heit in ei-ner Welt, in der nichts si-cher scheint. Gib mir in die-ser schwe-ren Zeit___ ir-gend-was, das___ bleibt.___ Gib mir ein-fach nur ein biss-chen Halt.

JOAN OF ARC
O.M.D.

♩ = 130	Waltz
Leadsound: Oboe	

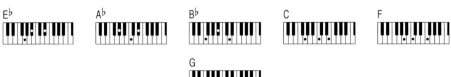

If Joan of Arc_____ had a

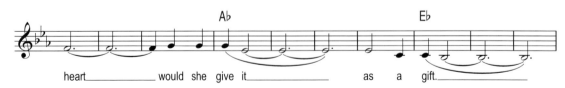

heat_____ would she give it_____ as a gift.

To such as me_____ who longs to see_____ how an

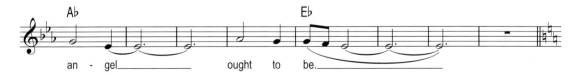

an - gel_____ ought to be._____

Her

dreams to give _____ her heart a - way _____ like an or - phan

_____ a - long the way. _____ She cared so much, _____

_ she of - fered up _____ her bod - y _____ to the

grave. _____

rep. ad lib.

JUNGLE DRUM
EMILIANA TORRINI

♩ = 118 | 8 Beat

Leadsound: Synth Lead

116

117

KEIN ZURÜCK
WOLFSHEIM

♩ = 82 | Pop Beat
Leadsound: Guitar

Musik & Text: Axel Ermes, Peter Heppner, Markus Reinhardt
© 2003 Hanseatic Musikverlag GmbH & Co KG. Warner/Chappell Overseas Holdings Limited, London.
Reproduced by permission of Faber Music Limited.
All Rights Reserved.

Es geht kein Weg zu-rück.

Weißt du noch, wie's war, Kin-der-zeit, wun-der-bar. Die Welt ist bunt und

schön. Bis du ir-gend-wann be-greifst, dass nicht je-der Ab-schied heißt,

es gibt auch ein Wie-der-sehn. Im-mer vor-wärts, Schritt um

Schritt. Es geht kein Weg zu-rück! Und was jetzt ist, wird nie mehr un-ge-schehn.

Die Zeit läuft uns da-von, was ge-tan ist, ist ge-tan. Was jetzt ist, wird

nie mehr so ge-schehn. Es geht kein Weg zu-rück.

Es geht kein Weg zu-rück. Ein Wort zu-viel im Zorn ge-sagt,

ein Schritt zu weit nach vorn ge - wagt: Schon ist es vor - bei.

Was auch im - mer ich jetzt ge - tan, was ich ge - sagt hab, ist ge - sagt,

Und was wie e - wig schien ist schon Ver - gang - en - heit.

Im - mer vor - wärts, Schritt um Schritt. Es geht kein Weg zu - rück!

Und was jetzt ist, wird nie mehr un - ge - schehn. Die Zeit läuft uns da - von,

was ge - tan ist, ist ge - tan. Was jetzt ist, wird nie mehr so ge - schehn.

Ach, und könnt ich doch nur ein einz - ges Mal die Uh - ren rück - wärts drehn.

Denn wie - viel von dem, was ich heu - te weiß, hätt ich lie - ber nie ge - sehn.

Es geht kein Weg zu - rück. Es geht kein Weg zu - rück.

Es geht__ kein Weg zu - rück.__ Dein Le - ben dreht__ sich nur im Kreis,

__ so voll von weg - ge - worf - 'ner Zeit,__ und dei - ne Träu - me schiebst du

end - los vor__ dir her.__ Du willst noch le - ben ir - gend - wann,

__ doch wenn nicht heu - te, wann denn dann, denn ir - gend - wann__ ist auch ein

Traum zu lan - ge her.__ Im - mer vor - wärts, Schritt um Schritt. Es geht__ kein Weg zu - rück!

__ Und was jetzt ist,__ wird nie mehr un - ge - schehn.__ Die Zeit läuft uns__ da - von,

__ was ge - tan__ ist, ist ge - tan.__ Was jetzt ist,__ wird nie mehr so__ ge - schehn.
Ach, und

könnt ich__ doch__ nur ein einz - ges__ Mal__ die Uh - ren__ rück - wärts drehn.

__ Denn wie - viel von__ dem,__ was ich heu - te__ weiß,__ hätt ich

lie - ber__ nie__ ge - sehn. Nie mehr so__ ge - schehn.__

KRIEGER DES LICHTS
SILBERMOND

♩ = 86 | 8 Beat

Leadsound: Flute

Musik & Text: Stefanie Kloss, Jan Andreas Nowak, Thomas Stolle, Johannes Stolle
© EMI Songs Musikverlag GmbH/ Valicon Songs oHG administered by EMI Songs Musikverlag GmbH /
Silbermond Musikverlag GmbH/Arabella Musikverlag GmbH (Universal Music Publishing Group).

Gsus² Bm Asus⁴ Em G

D

Sei wie der Fluss, der ei - sern ins

Meer fließt. Der sich nicht ab - brin - gen lässt, e - gal wie schwer es ist. Selbst den

größ - ten Stein_ fürch - tet er___ nicht. Auch wenn es Jah - re dau - ert, bis er ihn

bricht. Und wenn dein Wil - le schläft, dann weck ihn wie - der. Denn in

je - dem von uns__ steckt die - ser Krie - ger. Des - sen Mut ist wie ein

Schwert, doch die größ - te Waf - fe___ ist sein Herz.___ Lasst uns

121

auf - stehn. Macht euch auf den Weg. An al - le Krie - ger des Lichts.

An al - le Krie - ger des Lichts. Wo seid ihr, ihr seid ge-

braucht hier. Macht euch auf den Weg. An al - le Krie - ger des Lichts.

An al - le Krie - ger des Lichts. Das hier geht an

al - le Krie - ger des Lichts. Hab kei - ne

Angst vor dei - nen Schwä - chen. Fürch - te nie, dei - nen Feh - ler auf - zu - de - cken. Sei be-

dacht, be - ruhigt und be - freit. Sei auch ver - rückt von Zeit zu-

Zeit. Lass dich nicht täu - schen, auch wenn's aus Gold ist. Lass dich nicht

blen - den, erst recht von fal - schem Stolz nicht. Ler - ne ver - ge - ben und ver-

zeihn. Ler - ne zu fes - seln und zu be - frei - en. Lasst uns

al - le Krie - ger des Lichts.

Und er kennt sei - ne Gren - zen

und geht trotz - dem zu weit. Kein Glück in der Fer - ne,

nach dem er nicht greift. Sei - ne Macht ist sein Glau - be,

um nichts kämpft er mehr. Und das im - mer und im - mer wie - der,

des - we - gen ist er ein Krie - ger. Das ist ein Auf - ruf,

das hier geht an al - le Krie - ger, an al - le Krie - ger.

Das ist ein Auf - ruf. Und die - ser Auf - ruf geht

an al - le Krie - ger des Lichts. An al - le Krie - ger des Lichts. Das hier geht an

al - le Krie - ger des Lichts.

123

LET ME ENTERTAIN YOU
ROBBIE WILLIAMS

♩ = 124 | Rock Beat
Leadsound: Saxophone

Musik & Text: Robbie Williams & Guy Chambers

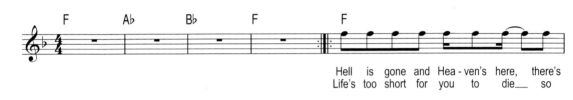

Hell is gone and Hea - ven's here, there's
Life's too short for you to die___ so

no thing left___ for you to fear,___ shake your ass, come ov - er here, now scream.
grab your - self___ an a - li - bi.___ Hea - ven knows your mo - ther lied, mon cher.

I'm a burn - ing ef - fi - gy___ of ev - 'ry - thing I used to be,
Se - pa - rate your right from wrongs, come and sing a diff - 'rent song the

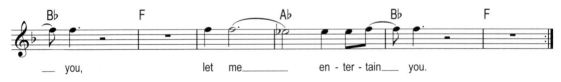

you're my rock of em - pa - thy, my dear. So come on let me___ en - ter - tain
ket - tle's on so don't be long, mon cher.

___ you, let me___ en - ter - tain___ you.

Look me up in the yel - low pa - ges I will be your rock of a - ges, you

see through fads and your cra - zy pha - ses, yeah.

Little Bo Peep has lost his sheep, he popped a pill and fell a-sleep, the

dew is wet but the grass is sweet, my dear. Your mind gets burned with the
He may be good, he may be

ha-bits you've learned, but we're the ge-ne-ra - tion that's got to be heard. You're
out - ta sight,_ but he can't be here so come a - round to - night._

tired of your tea-chers and your school's a drag,_ you're not going to end_ up like your
Here is the place where the feel-ing grows, you've got-ta get high_ be-fore you

mum and dad._ So come on... Let me_____ en-ter - tain you.
taste the lows._ So come on...

Let me_____ en-ter- tain__ you.

(improvise ad lib.)

Come on, come on, come on,_ come on,_ come on, come on, come on,_ come on,_

come on, come on, come on,_come on._____

Let me en-ter - tain__ you, let me en-ter - tain__ you.

repeat ad lib. and fade out

125

LOVE AT FIRST SIGHT
KYLIE MINOGUE

♩ = 125 | Disco Beat
Leadsound: Flute

Musik & Text: Kylie Minogue, Martin Harrington, Richard Stannard, Julian Gallagher & Ash Howes
© Copyright 2001 Universal Music Publishing Limited. All rights in Germany administered by Universal Music Publ. GmbH /
Sony/ATV Music Publishing (UK) Limited/ /EMI Music Publishing Limited/ Mushroom Music PTY Limited/ Biffco Music Publishing Limited
Alle Rechte für Deutschland, Österreich, Schweiz GLOBAL MUSIKVERLAG, München.
All Rights Reserved. International Copyright Secured.

127

MAD WORLD
TEARS FOR FEARS

♩ = 118 | 8 Beat

Leadsound: Vibraphone

Musik & Text: Roland Orzabal
© Chrysalis Music Limited. Alle Rechte für Deutschland, Österreich, Schweiz GLOBAL MUSIKVERLAG, München.

All a-round me are fa - mil - iar fa - ces, worn out pla - ces,
Chil - dren wait - ing for the day they feel__ good, Hap - py Birth - day,

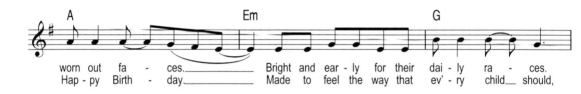

worn out fa - ces._____ Bright and ear - ly for their dai - ly ra - ces.
Hap - py Birth - day._____ Made to feel the way that ev' - ry child__ should,

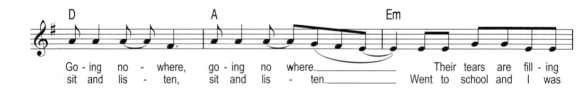

Go - ing no - where, go - ing no where._____ Their tears are fill - ing
sit and lis - ten, sit and lis - ten._____ Went to school and I was

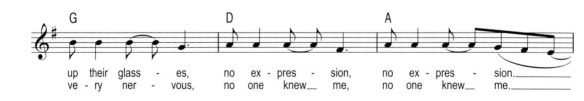

up their glass - es, no ex - pres - sion, no ex - pres - sion._____
ve - ry ner - vous, no one knew__ me, no one knew__ me._____

__ Hide my head I want to drown my sor - row,
__ Hel - lo tea - cher tell me what's my les - son,

no to - mor - row, no to - mor - row.
look right through me, look right through me.

And I find it kin - da fun - ny, I find it kin - da

sad. The dreams in which I'm dy - ing are the best I've ev - er had. I find it hard to

tell you, I find it hard to take when peo - ple run in cir - cles. It's a ve - ry, ve - ry

mad world, mad world. mad world,

mad world.

D.S. al CODA

En - large your world. mad world.

129

MERCY
DUFFY

♩ = 128	8 Beat
Leadsound: Saxophone	

Musik & Text: Duffy & Stephen Booker
© Copyright 2007 EMI Music Publishing Limited. Reproduced by permission of International Music Publications Limited (a trading
name of Faber Music Limited) / Universal Music Publishing Limited (administered in Germany by Universal Music Publishing GmbH).
All Rights Reserved. International Copyright Secured.

Yeah, yeah, yeah.

Yeah, yeah, yeah.

I love you

but I got-ta stay true.
will be some-thing on the side.

My mo-rals got me on my
But you got to un-der-

knees, I'm begg-ing please stop play-ing games.
stand that I need a man who can take my hand.

I don't know what this is but you got me good just like you knew you would.

I don't know what you do but you do it well,

I'm un-der your spell. You got me begg-ing you for

NEW SOUL
YAEL NAIM

♩ = 100	Pop Beat
	Leadsound: Piano

Musik & Text: Yael / Arranged by David Donatien
© 2007 Lili Louise Musique Sarl
Warner/Chappell Overseas Holdings Limited, London. Reproduced by permission of Faber Music Limited.
All Rights Reserved.

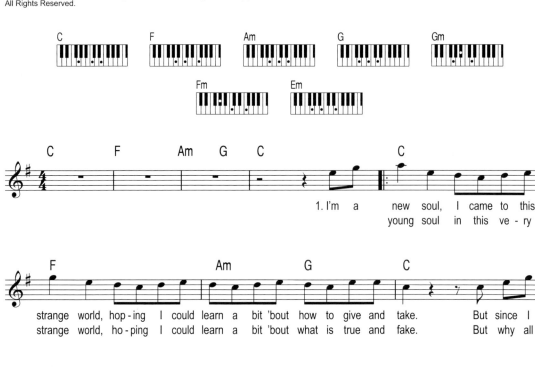

1. I'm a new soul, I came to this
   young soul in this ve-ry

strange world, hop-ing I could learn a bit 'bout how to give and take. But since I
strange world, ho-ping I could learn a bit 'bout what is true and fake. But why all

came here, felt the joy and the fear, find-ing my-self mak-ing ev-'ry pos-sib-le mis-
this hate? Try to com-mu-ni-cate, fin-ding trust and love is not al-ways ea-sy to

take. La-la la la la-la la-la la la la-la la-la. La la-la la la-la
make.

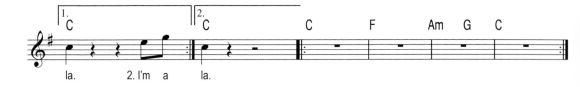

la. La-la la la la-la la-la la la la-la la-la. La la-la la la-la

1.
C
la. 2. I'm a

2.
C   C   F   Am G C
la.

This is a hap - py end,_____ cause you don't un - der - stand,___

ev - 'ry - thing you__ have done,_____ why's ev - 'ry - thing_ so wrong?____

This is a hap - py end,__ come and give me your hand, I'll take you far__ a - way.

___ I'm a new soul, I came to this strange world, hop - ing I could

learn a bit 'bout how to give and take. But since I came here, felt the joy and

the fear, find - ing my - self mak - ing ev - 'ry pos - sib - le mis - take. La - la

la la la - la la - la la la la - la la - la. La la - la la la - la la. La - la

la la la - la la - la la la la - la la - la. La la - la la la - la la

la. La - la
(last time tacet)

NICHTS PASSIERT
SILBERMOND

♩ = 156 | Rock Beat

Leadsound: E-Guitar

Musik & Text: Stefanie Kloss, Andreas Jan Nowak, Johannes Stolle, Thomas Stolle
© EMI Songs Musikverlag GmbH/ Valicon Songs oHG adm. by EMI Songs Musikverlag GmbH / Silbermond Musikverlag GmbH / Arabella Musikverlag GmbH (Universal Music Publishing Group).

Die Wor - te wei - se ge - wählt,__ von de - nen nach - her

keins mehr zählt.. Passt auf,__ dass ihr euch nicht ver - sprecht,__ bei den Ver - spre - chen, die ihr

__ brecht. Das klingt nach Schall und nach Rauch, wie ihr eu - re

Sät - ze baut. Wer's glaubt,__ wird se - lig, a - ber Se - li - ge seh ich hier nicht.__

Und ich frag mich, wie-viel Zeit wollt ihr denn noch ver-liern. Ich

seh euch im-mer re-den, a-ber nichts pas-siert. Al-so sagt mir, wie-viel

Zeit wollt ihr denn noch ver-liern. Ihr seid die gan-ze Zeit am re-den, a-ber

nichts pas-siert.

Sind eu-re Lei-chen ver-steckt, so gut, dass man sie nie ent-deckt? Es ist

nur ei-ne Fra-ge der Zeit,__ bis ihr die Schla-fen-den weckt.__ Kommt doch mal

run-ter für__ mich und seht die Welt aus un-s'rer Sicht.__ Hier ist nur

Sicht-ba-res Wah-res, doch in Sicht ist hier lei-der nichts.__ Und ich

D.S. al CODA

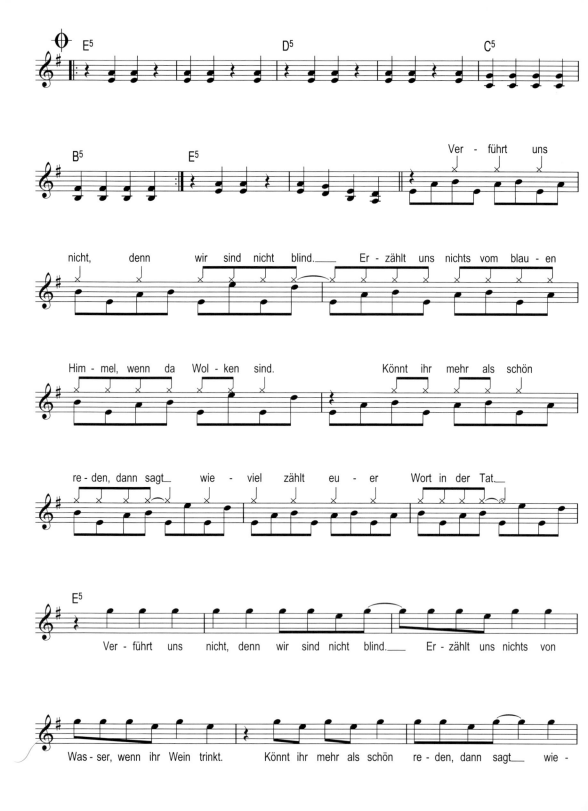

Ver - führt uns nicht, denn wir sind nicht blind.___ Er - zählt uns nichts vom blau - en Him - mel, wenn da Wol - ken sind. Könnt ihr mehr als schön re - den, dann sagt___ wie - viel zählt eu - er Wort in der Tat___

Ver - führt uns nicht, denn wir sind nicht blind.___ Er - zählt uns nichts von Was - ser, wenn ihr Wein trinkt. Könnt ihr mehr als schön re - den, dann sagt___ wie -

-viel zählt eu - er Wort in der Tat___ Ver - führt uns nicht, denn wir sind nicht blind.

G5

Er - zählt uns nichts vom blau - en Him - mel, wenn da Wol - ken sind.

A5

Ein Wort al - lein hat noch kei - nen Stein ge - dreht und es ist Zeit, dass sich was be - wegt.

Dsus2   E5   A5

Und ich frag mich, wie - viel Zeit wollt ihr denn noch ver - liern. Ich

G5   E5

seh euch im - mer re - den, a - ber nichts pas - siert. Al - so sagt mir, wie - viel

A5   C5   Eb5

Zeit wollt ihr denn noch ver - liern. Ihr seid die gan - ze Zeit am re - den, die

E5   A5   C5   Eb5   E5

gan - ze Zeit am re - den, re - den, re - den. Nichts pas - siert.

D5

C#5

E5

137

NUR EIN WORT
WIR SIND HELDEN

♩ = 186 | Pop Beat

Leadsound: Flute

Musik: Judith Holofernes, Jean-Michel Tourette, Pola Roy, Mark Tavassol / Text: Judith Holofernes
© Wintrup / Freudenhaus.

Ich se- -he, dass du denkst, ich den - ke, dass du fühlst, ich füh - le, dass du willst, a - ber ich hör___ dich nicht, ich hab mir ein Wör - ter - buch ge - liehen, dir A bis Z ins Ohr ge - schrien. Ich sta - pel tau - send wir - re Wor - te auf,___ die dich am Är - mel ziehen. Und wo du hin - gehen willst, ich häng an dei - nen Bei - nen, wenn du schon auf den Mund fal - len musst, wa - rum dann nicht auf mei - nen. Oh, bit - te gib___ mir nur ein Oh, bit - te gib___ mir nur ein Oh, bit - te gib___ mir nur ein, bit - te, bit - te gib___ mir nur ein Wort.

138

Es ist ver-rückt, wie schön du schweigst, wie du dein hüb-sches Köpf-chen

neigst, und so der gan-zen lau-ten Welt und mir die kal-te Schul-ter

zeigst. Dein Schwei-gen ist dein Zelt, du stellst es mit-ten in die Welt, spannst die

Schnü-re und staunst stumm, wenn nachts ein Mäd-chen drü-ber fällt. Zu dei-nen

Fü-ßen red ich mich um Kopf und Kra-gen, ich

will in dei-ne tie-fen Was-ser gro-ße Wel-len schla-gen.

In mei-nem Blut wer-fen die En-dor-phi-ne Bla-sen, wenn hin-ter dei-nen

stil-len Ha-sen-au-gen die Ge-dan-ken ra-sen. Oh, bit-te gib mir nur ein

Oh, bit-te gib mir nur ein Oh, bit-te gib mir nur ein,

bit-te, bit-te gib mir nur ein Wort.

139

ONE DAY IN YOUR LIFE
ANASTACIA

♩ = 118 | Rock Beat

Leadsound: Flute

Musik & Text: Anastacia, Sam Watters & Louis Biancaniello
© Copyright 2001 Poho Productions / Universal Music Corporation / Breakthrough Creations/ S.M.Y. Publishing / Sony/ATV Tunes
LLC, USA. Sony/ATV Music Publishing (UK) Limited / Universal/MCA Music Limited.
All rights in Germany administered by Universal/MCA Music Publishing GmbH.
All Rights Reserved. International Copyright Secured.

Em   D   C   Bm   D#dim

Am   G   A

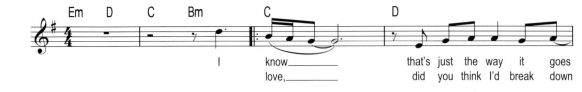

I know____ that's just the way it goes
love,____ did you think I'd break down

___ and you ain't right.____ For sure____ you turned your back on love
___ and cry.____ This thing we had,__ it meant the world to me,

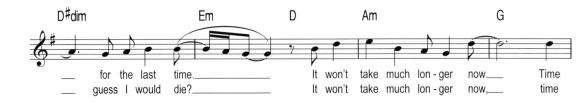

___ for the last time.____ It won't take much lon-ger now.__ Time
___ guess I would die?____ It won't take much lon-ger now,__ time

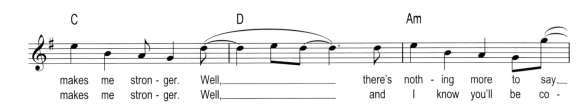

makes me stron-ger. Well,_____ there's noth-ing more to say.__
makes me stron-ger. Well,_____ and I know you'll be co-

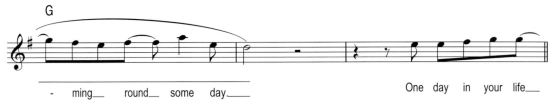

- ming__ round__ some day.____

One day in your life__

140

say love will re-mind____ you, how could you leave____ it all be-hind..

____ One day in your life_____ it's gon-na find____ you with the tears that left___ me cry.

____ And ba-by I'm stron-ger than__ be-fore,____ you got - ta play it on___ the line.

_____ May-be one day in your life.____ FINE My

You called me in____ the mid-night hour_____ with your weav - y lies____

so man - y sleep - less nights.__ I won - der_____

D.S. al FINE

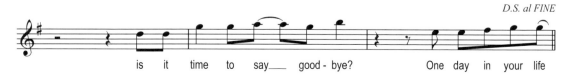

is it time to say___ good - bye? One day in your life

PAPARAZZI
LADY GAGA

Musik & Text: Stefanie Germanotta, Robert Fusari

♩= 115 | 8 Beat

Leadsound: Synth Lead

We are the crowd, we're co - com - ing out.__ Got my
I'll be a girl__ back - stage at your show, vel - vet

flash on, it's true,_ need that pic - ture of you.__ It's so mag - i - cal.__ We'd be so fan-
ropes and gui - tars._ Yeah, cause you're my rock - star_ in - be - tween the sets, eye - lin - er and

-tas - ti - cal.__ Leath - er and jeans, ga - rage glam - or - ous.__ Not
cig - a - rettes. Shad - ow is burned, yel - low dance and re - turn.__ My

sure what it means, but this pho - to of us,__ it don't have a price. Read - y for those
lash - es are dry,__ pur - ple tear - drops I cry.__ It don't have a price. Lov - ing you is

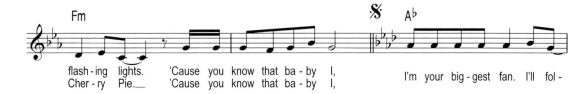

flash - ing lights. 'Cause you know that ba - by I, I'm your big - gest fan. I'll fol-
Cher - ry Pie.__ 'Cause you know that ba - by I,

- low you un - til you love__ me, Pa - pa,__ Pa - pa - raz - zi.__

Ba - by there's no oth - er su - per - star, you know that I'll___ be___ your Pa - pa,___

Pa - pa - raz - zi.___ Prom - ise I'll be___ kind,___ but I won't stop un -

- til that boy is___ mine.___ Ba - by you'll be fa - mous. Chase

___ you down un - til you love___ me.___ Pa - pa,___ Pa - pa - raz - zi.___

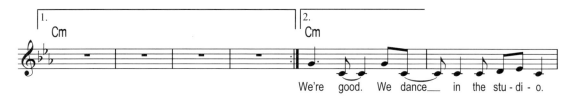

We're good. We dance___ in the stu - di - o.

Snap, snap,_ that shit___ on the ra - di - o. Don't stop for an - y - one.___

We're plas - tic but we still have fun!

POKER FACE
LADY GAGA

Musik & Text: Stefani Germanotta & Nadir Khayat
© Copyright 2008 Sony/ATV Music Publishing (UK) Limited.
All Rights Reserved. International Copyright Secured.

♩ = 118	Disco Beat
	Leadsound: Vibraphone

I wan-na hold 'em like they do in Tex-as, please. Fold 'em let 'em hit me, raise it
mah). I wan-na roll with him, a hard pair we will be. A lit-tle gam-bl-ing is

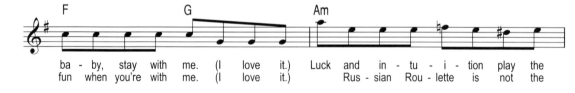

ba-by, stay with me. (I love it.) Luck and in-tu-i-tion play the
fun when you're with me. (I love it.) Rus-sian Rou-lette is not the

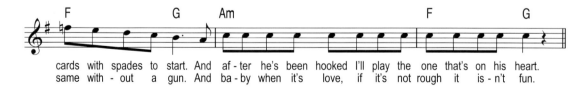

cards with spades to start. And af-ter he's been hooked I'll play the one that's on his heart.
same with-out a gun. And ba-by when it's love, if it's not rough it is-n't fun.

Oh, oh, oh, oh, oh, oh-oh-e-oh-oh-oh. I'll get him hot, show him what I've got.___

145

PRECIOUS
DEPECHE MODE

♩ = 105 | Pop Beat
Leadsound: Piano

Musik & Text: Martin Gore

1. Pre-cious_ and fra-gile things_ need spe-cial hand-ling._
2. An-gels_ with sil-ver wings_ should-n't_ know suf-fer-ing._

My God_ what have we done_ to you?_ We al-ways
I wish I_ could take the pain_ for you._ If God has_ a

try to share the ten-der-est of care._ Now look_ what
mas-ter plan_ that on-ly_ He un-der stands, I hope it's_ your

we have put_ you through._ Things get da-maged, things get
eyes he's see-ing through._

bro-ken, I thought we'd man-age but words left_ un-spo-ken, left us_ so

brit - tle, there was__ so lit - tle left__ to give.__

I pray__ you learn to trust, have faith__ in both of us.__ And keep__ room in your hearts for two.__

Things get da - maged, things get bro - ken, I thought we'd man - age but words left__ un - spo - ken, left us__ so brit - tle, there was__ so lit - tle left__ to give.__

PRIDE (IN THE NAME OF LOVE)

U2

♩ = 106 | 8 Beat

Leadsound: Saxophone

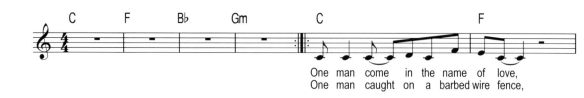

One man come in the name of love,
One man caught on a barbed wire fence,

one man come and go.___
one man he re - sists.___

One man come here to jus - ti - fy,___
One man washed on an emp - ty beach,

one man to o - ver - throw.___
one man be - trayed with a kiss.

In the name___ of love,___ one man

_ in the name of love._ In the name_ of love,____ what more?

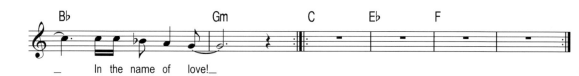

_ In the name of love!_

Mmh, mh, mh___ mh, mh, mh, mh,___ mh,

mh, mh, mh,___ mh, mh.   Ear - ly mor - ning,   A - pril four

shot rings out___ in the Mem - phis sky._____   Free at last,   they took your life,___ they

could not take your pride.___   In the name_____ of love,___   one man

___ in the name of love.___   In the name___ of love,_____ what more?

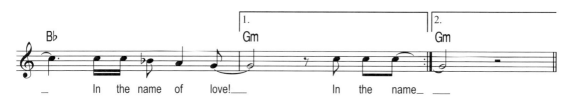

___ In the name of love!___   In the name___ ___

Oh, oh, oh,   oh, oh, oh, oh,   oh, oh, oh, oh,   oh, oh, oh, oh,   oh.

ROCKFERRY
DUFFY

♩ = 88　8 Beat

Leadsound: Strings

Musik & Text: Aimee Ann Duffy, Bernard Joseph Butler
© 2006 EMI Music Publishing Limited and Stage Three Music Limited. EMI Music Publishing Limited, London.
Reproduced by permission of International Music Publications Limited (a trading name of Faber Music Limited).
Rechte für D/A/CH Wintrup Musikverlag. All Rights Reserved.

D　　C　　G　　F

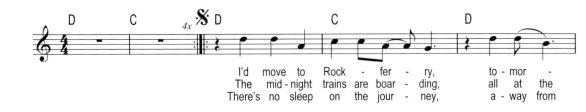

I'd move to Rock - fer - ry, to - mor -
The mid - night trains are boar - ding, all at the
There's no sleep on the jour - ney, a - way from

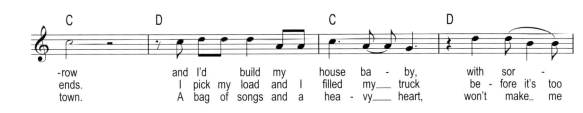

-row and I'd build my house ba - by, with sor -
ends. I pick my load and I filled my__ truck be - fore it's too
town. A bag of songs and a hea - vy__ heart, won't make_ me

- row. I'll leave my sha - dow,_____ to fall___ be -
late. I leave the stars to judge,_____ my ev - 'ry__
doubt. I give it all___ my__ strength and my__ mind,

- hind. And I would - n't write____ to you,___
___ move. I'm not go - ing to think____ of you___
_____ I'll make this de - ci - sion,_____

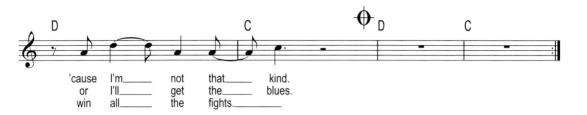

'cause I'm____ not that____ kind.
or I'll____ get the____ blues.
win all____ the fights.____

There's no____ sleep__ on the jour - ney, a - way__ from town.__

A bag of songs and a heav - y heart, won't make_ me doubt.__

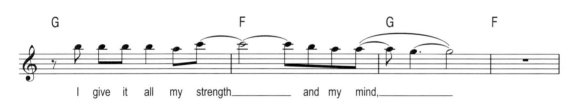

I give it all my strength____ and my mind,____

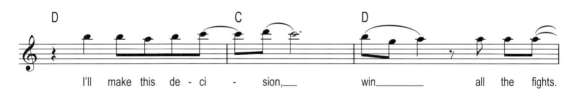

I'll make this de - ci - sion,__ win____ all the fights.

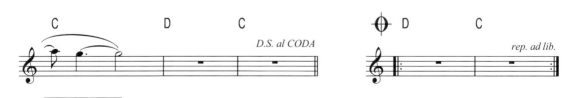

D.S. al CODA

rep. ad lib.

151

RUBY
KAISER CHIEFS

♩ = 94 | 8 Beat

Leadsound: Flute

Musik & Text: Nicholas Hodgson, Richard Wilson, Andrew White, James Rix & Nicholas Baines
© Copyright 2006 Rondor Music (London) Limited. All rights in Germany administered by Rondor Musikverlag GmbH.
All Rights Reserved. International Copyright Secured.

D   Am   Em   Bm   D#dim

C

Let it

nev-er be said,_ the ro-mance is dead_ 'cos there's so lit-tle else_ oc-cu-
lack of in-t'rest_ to-mor-row's can-celed. Let the clocks be re-set_ and the

-py-ing my head. There is noth-ing I need_ ex-cept the func-tion to breathe but I'm
pen-du-lums held._ 'Cos there's noth-ing at all_ ex-cept the space in bet-ween._ Fin-ding

not real-ly fussed, does-n't mat-ter to me._
out what you're called_ and re-peat-ing your name.

Ru-by, Ru-by, Ru-by,

Ru - by.__ Ah._____ And do ya, do ya, do ya, do ya?__ Ah._____

__ Know what ya do - ing, do - ing to me?__ Ah._____

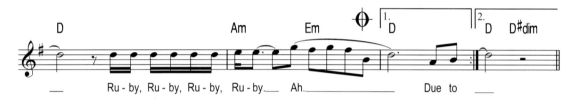

__ Ru - by, Ru - by, Ru - by, Ru - by.__ Ah._____ Due to __

Could it be, could it be that you're jok - ing with me__ and you
(3. + 4.x instr.)

don't real - ly see__ you with me._____ Ru - by, Ru - by, Ru - by,

__ And do ya, do ya, do ya, do ya?__ Ah._____

__ Know what ya do - ing, do - ing to me?__ Ah._____

153

RUN TO YOU
BRYAN ADAMS

♩ = 128	Rock Beat
Leadsound: Saxophone	

Musik & Text: Bryan Adams & Jim Vallance
© Copyright 1984 Adams Communications Incorporated/ Testatyme Music, USA.
Universal Music Publishing Limited. All rights in Germany administered by Universal Music Publ. GmbH.
All Rights Reserved. International Copyright Secured.

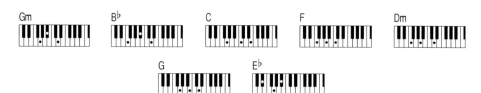

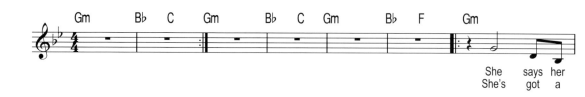

She says her
She's got a

love for me___ could nev-er die. But that would change if she
heart of gold, she'd ne-ver let me down. But you're the wo-man that al-

ev-er found out a-bout you and I. Oh, but her
ways turns me on, you keep me co-ming round. I know her

love is cold. It would-n't hurt her if she did-n't know, cause when it
love is true but it's so damn ea-sy ma-king love to you. I got my

gets too much I need to feel your touch.
mind made up,___ I need to feel your touch. I'm gon-na

RHYTHM IS A DANCER
SNAP

♩ = 124	Disco Beat
Leadsound: Synth Lead	

Musik & Text: Thea Austin, Benito Benites, D. Butler & John Garrett III

Rhy - thm is a dan - cer,___ it's___ a source com - pa - nion, peo - ple feel it ev - 'ry where.

___ Lift your hands and voi - ces,___ free___ your mind and join us,___

you can feel it in the air._____ Oh oh it's a pas - sion,_ oh

oh, you can feel it___ in the air. Oh oh it's a

pas - sion,__ oh oh oh oh oh oh,___ oh, oh.___

SATELLITE
LENA

♩ = 180 | Pop Beat

Leadsound: Flute

Musik & Text: Julie Frost, John Gordon

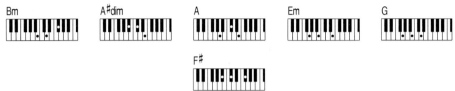

I went ev - 'ry - where_ for you,_ I e - ven did_ my hair_ for you._ I

bought new un - der - wear,_they're blue_ and I wore 'em just the oth - er day._

Love, you know I'll fight_ for you,_ I left on the_ porch light_ for you.

Wheth - er you are sweet or cruel_ I'm gon - na love you_ ei - ther way._

Love, oh, love,_____ I got - ta tell you how I feel a - bout_____ you. 'Cause I,_

__ oh, I____ can't_ go a mi - nute with - out_ your love._

Like a sat - el - lite,_ I'm_ in an or - bit all the way a - round_____ you. And I would

fall out in-to the night,___ can't go a mi-nute with-out___ your love.___

Em   A   Bm

Love, I got it bad___ for you,___ I saved the best___ I have

A#dim   A

___ for you.___ You some-times make me sad___ and blue___ would-n't have it an-y___ oth-er way.

Bm   A#dim   A

___ Love, my aim is straight___ and true,___ cu-pid's ar-row is just___

Bm   A#dim   A

___ for you.___ I e-ven pain-ted my toe nails___ for you,___ I did it just the___ o-ther day.

Bm   Em   A

___ Love, oh, love,_____ I got-ta tell you how I feel a-bout

Bm   Em   A

_____ you. 'Cause I,___ oh, I___ can't go a mi-nute with-out___ your love.

Bm   Em   A

___ Like a sat-el-lite,___ I'm___ in an or - bit all the way a-round

Bm   Em   A

_____ you.___ And I would fall out in-to the night,___ can't go a mi-nute with-out___ your

Bm   Em   A   Bm

love, oh, love,_____ I got-ta tell you how I feel a-bout_____ you. 'Cause I,

Em   A   Bm

___ oh, I___ can't go a mi-nute with-out___ your love.___

SECRETS
ONE REPUBLIC

♩ = 74 | 8 Beat

Leadsound: Flute

Musik & Text: Ryan Tedder
© Copyright 2009 Write 2 Live Publishing / Sony/ATV Tunes LLC / Velvet Hammer Music, USA.
Sony/ATV Music Publishing (UK) Limited.

I need an-oth-er sto-ry, some-thing to get off my chest.__ My life gets kind of bor-ing, need some-thing that I can con-fess. Till all my sleaves are stained red,__ from all the truth that I've said.__ Come by it hon-est-ly I swear, thought you saw me wink, no, I've been on the brink, so. Tell me what you want to hear, some-thing that will like those ears. Sick of all the in-sin-cere, so I'm gon-na give all my se-crets a-way.__ This time,__ don't need an-oth-er per-fect line, don't care if cri-tics ne-ver jump in line.__ I'm gon-na give all my se-crets a-way.

SHE SAID
PLAN B.

♩ = 148 | Pop Beat
Leadsound: Flute

She said I love you boy, I love you so.

She said, I love you ba - by, oh oh oh oh.

She said I love you more than words can say. She said I love you ba-

-a - a - a - a - by.

So I said, what you say - ing girl it can't be right.

How can you be in love with me? We on - ly just met to - night.

So she said, boy I loved you from the start

when I first heard love goes down some - thing star - ted burn - ing in my heart.

I said stop this cra - zy talk_____ and leave right

now and close the door._____ She said, but I love you boy, I love you so.__

She said, I love you ba - by oh oh oh oh._____

She said, I love you more than words can say.__ She said, I love you ba -

-a - a - a - a - by._____

(Rap): So now up in the courts pleading my case in a witness box telling the judge and jur' the same thing that I said to the cops. On the day that I got arrested I'm innocent I protested, she just feels rejected had her heart book on mine someone she's obsessed with. She likes sign on my music, she makes out a fan of my music, so I love them diamonds to lose itcos she can't stop and read the man from the music. And I'm saying all this from the stand but my girl cries tears from the galleries got bigger than I ever could have planned like that song about the Zuton Valerie.

D.C. al CODA

(Rap. cont.): So the jury don't look like their buying it and she's making me nervous, and I'm just screw faced like I'm trying it their eyes fixed on me like I'm murderous. They wanna lock me up and throw away the key, they wanna send me down even though I told them she...

I said why the hell you got - ta treat me this way._____ You don't know what love_ is.__

__ You would - n't do this if you__ did.__ No, no,_ no. Mh.__

SHOUT
TEARS FOR FEARS

♩ = 130 | 8 Beat

Leadsound: Saxophone

Gm Eb Cm Bb Csus²

As cold as ice, I hope we live to tell the tale.

I hope we live to... Shout, shout, let it all out, these are the things I can

do with - out. Come on, I'm talk - ing to you, come on.

N.C. C(sus2)

Gm

Shout, shout, let it all out, these are the things I can do with - out. Come on,

I'm talk - ing to you, come on.

And when you've ta - ken down your guard. If I

could change your mind, I'd real - ly love to break your heart.

I'd real - ly love to... Shout, shout, let it all out, these are the things I can

do with- out. Come on, I'm talk - ing to you, come on.

SMOOTH
SANTANA FEAT. ROB THOMAS

♩ = 116	Latin Beat
Leadsound: E-Guitar	

Musik & Text: Itaal Shur and Robert Thomas
© 1999 Itaal Shur Music, Warner Tamerlane Publishing Corporation, U Rule Music Inc and EMI Blackwood Music Incorporated.
Warner/Chappell North America Limited / EMI Music Publishing Limited. Reproduced by permission of Faber Music Limited.
All Rights Reserved. International Copyright Secured.

SO WHAT
PINK

♩ = 126 | 12/8 Beat

Leadsound: Flute

Musik & Text: Alecia Moore, Max Martin, Johan Schuster
© 2008 Pink Inside Publishing and Maratone AB, Sweden.
Kobalt Music Publishing Limited / EMI Music Publishing Limited, London. Reproduced by permission of
International Music Publications Limited (a trading name of Faber Music Limited). All Rights Reserved.

Na, na, na, na, na, na, na,

na, na, na, na, na, na. 1. I guess I just lost my hus - band
(1.x tacet) wai - ter just took my ta - ble and

I don't know where he went. So I'm gon - na drink my mo - ney, I'm
gave it to Jes - si - ca Simps. I guess I'll go sit with drum boy at

not gon - na pay his rent. I got a brand new at - ti - tude and
least he'll know how to hit. What if this song's on the ra - di - o? Then

I'm gon - na wear it to - night. I'm gon - na get in trou - ble, I wan - na start a fight.
some - bo - dy's gon - na die. I'm gon - na get in trou - ble, my ex will start a fight.

Na, na, na, na, na, na, na, I wan - na start a fight.
Na, na, na, na, na, na, na, he's gon - na start a fight.

Na, na, na, na, na, na, na, I wan - na start a fight. So, so what, I'm still a
Na, na, na, na, na, na, na, yeah, he's gon - na get in a fight.

rock star, I got my rock moves and I don't need you.__ And guess what, I'm hav - in'

more fun   and now that we're done   I'm gon-na show   you   to-night.___   I'm al-right,

___   I'm just fine___   and you're a fool.   So,   so what,   I am a rock star,   I got my

rock moves   and I don't want   you   to-night.___   2. The

You_ were-n't___ there,___ you_ nev-er___ were.   You_ want_ it___ all___

___ but_ that's not_ fair.___ I_ gave_ you_ life,___ I_ gave_ my_ all._

___ You_ were-n't___ there,___ you_ let_ me_ fall.___   So

so what,   I'm still a rock star,   I got my rock moves   and I don't need   you.___ And

guess what,   I'm hav-in' more fun   and now that we're done   I'm gon-na show you to-night.

___   I'm al-right,___   I'm just fine___   and you're a fool.   So,   so what,   I am a

rock star,   I got my rock moves   and I don't want   you   to-night._____

SOLDIER OF LOVE
SADE

♩ = 90	Slow Beat
Leadsound: Vibraphone	

Text: Sade Adu / Musik: Sade Adu, Andrew Hale, Stuart Matthewman & Paul Denman
© Copyright 2010 Angel Music Limited. Sony/ATV Music Publishing.
All Rights Reserved. International Copyright Secured.

 Gm
 Cm
 Gm♭6
 D

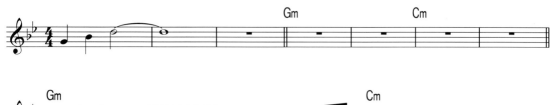

I've lost the use of my heart___ but I'm___ still a-live.

Still look-ing for__ the life, and the end-less_ pool on the oth-er

side._____ It's a wild wild west, I'm do-ing my best.

I'm at the bor-der-line_ of my___faith, I'm at the hin-ter-land_ of my de-

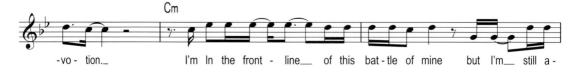

-vo-tion._ I'm In the front-line__ of this bat-tle of mine but I'm__ still a-

live. I'm a sol-dier of love. Ev'-ry day__ and

night._____ I'm a sol-dier of love. All the days_ of

SUCH A SHAME
TALK TALK

♩ = 114 | 8 Beat

Leadsound: Saxophone

Musik & Text: Mark Hollis
© Copyright 1984 Island Music Limited. Universal/Island Music Limited.
All rights in Germany administered by Universal Music Publishing GmbH.
All Rights Reserved. International Copyright Secured.

Such a shame to be-lieve___ in es-cape,

a life___ on ev-'ry face.___ And that's a change___
de-cide my fate.___ And that's a shame.___

till I'm f - inal-ly left___ with an eight.___ Tell me to re-lax, I just stare.
In these trembl - ing___ hands my___ faith.___ Tells me to re-act, I don't care.

___ May-be I don't___ know if I should change.___ A feel-ing that we
___ May-be it's un - kind that I should change.___ A feel-ing that we

share. It's a shame.___ Such a shame.___
share.

Num - ber me with rage.___ It's a shame.___ Such a shame.___

Num - ber me in haste.___ Such a shame. This ea - ger-ness to a change.

172

SWEET ABOUT ME
GABRIELLA CILMI

♩ = 130 | Shuffle

Leadsound: Flute

Musik & Text: Gabriella Cilmi, Miranda Cooper, Brian Higgins, Timothy Powell, Tim Larcombe, Nick Coler
© 2007 Biscottini Pty Limited, Warner/Chappell Music Limited and Xenomania Songs Limited.
EMI Music Publishing Limited, London. Warner/Chappell Music Limited, London. Warner/Chappell Music Publishing Limited, London.
Reproduced by permission of International Music Publications Limited
(a trading name of Faber Music Limited) and Faber Music Limited. All Rights Reserved.

Ooh,___ watch - ing me,___ hang - ing by a string this time.___

Don't ea - si - ly, cli - max of the per - fect lie.___

If there's les - sons to be learned,___ I'd ra - ther get my jamm - ing

words in first so. Tell you some - thing that I've found,___ that the
When you're play - ing with de - sire,___ don't come

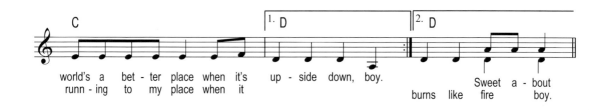

world's a bet - ter place when it's up - side down, boy.
runn - ing to my place when it

burns like fire boy. Sweet a - bout

me,   noth - ing   sweet_   a - bout   me,   yeah._____   Sweet a - bout

me,   noth - ing   sweet_   a - bout   me,   yeah._____   Sweet a - bout

me,   noth - ing   sweet_   a - bout   me,   yeah._____   Sweet a - bout

me,   noth - ing   sweet_   a - bout   me,   yeah._____

FINE

Blue,   blue,__   blue,_____   waves   they__   crash__   as
Too,   too__   smooth,__   ain't   all__   that,__   why

D.S. al FINE

time   goes__   by,_____   so   hard   to__   catch.__
don't   you__   ride_____   my   side   of__   the   track.

SWEET DREAMS (ARE MADE OF THIS)   EURYTHMICS

♩ = 125	Pop Beat
Leadsound: Strings	

Sweet dreams are made__ of this,__

who am__ I__ to dis - a - gree? I trav - el the world and the sev - en seas.

Ev - 'ry - bod - y's look - ing for some - thing. Some of them want to use__ you.

Some of them want to get used__ by you.__ Some of them want to a - buse__ you.

Some of them want to be__ a - bused.__

Sweet dreams are made__ of this,__

who am__ I__ to dis - a - gree? I trav - el the world and the

sev - en seas.___ Ev - 'ry - bod - y's look - ing for some - thing.

Hold your head up. Keep your head up, mov - in' on.___

Hold your head up, mov - in' on.___ Keep your head up, mov - in' on.___

Hold your head up, mov - in' on.___ Keep your head up, mov - in' on.___

Hold your head up, mov - in' on.___ Keep your head up.

Sweet dreams are made___ of this,___ who am___ I___ to dis - a - gree? I

trav - el the world and the sev - en seas. Ev - 'ry - bod - y's look - ing for some - thing.

THE WORLD IS NOT ENOUGH
GARBAGE

♩ = 86 | 8 Beat

Leadsound: Strings

Text: Don Black / Musik: David Arnold
© Copyright 1999 United Lion Music Incorporated, USA.
Sony/ATV Music Publishing (UK) Limited.
All Rights Reserved. International Copyright Secured.

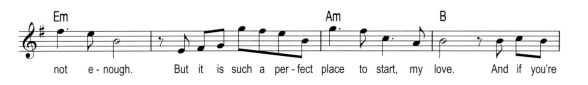

not e-nough. But it is such a per-fect place to start, my love. And if you're

strong e-nough to-ge-ther we can take the world a-part, my love.

I feel safe. I feel scared. I feel

read - y and yet un-pre - pared. The world is

not e-nough. But it is such a per-fect place to start, my love. And if you're

strong e-nough to-ge-ther we can take the world a-part, my love. The world is

not e - nough. The world is not e - nough. No no-where

near e - nough, The world is not e - nough._____

THERE MUST BE AN ANGEL
EURYTHMICS

♩ = 112 | Pop Beat

Leadsound: Vibraphone

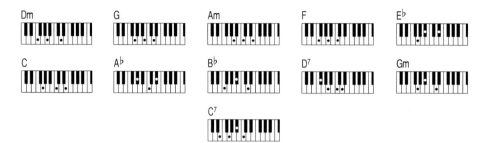

Da - da - da - da - da - da - da - da, da - da, da - da.

Da - da - da - da - da - da - da - da, da - da, da - da. Yeah.

No - one on earth_ could feel like this,
this,
I'm thrown and o - ver - blown with
I'm thrown and o - ver - blown with

bliss._____ There must be an an - gel_ play - ing with my_
bliss._____ There must be an an - gel_ play - ing with my_

_ heart,_ yeah._ I walk in - to_ an emp - ty room,_
_ heart,_ yeah._ And when I think_ that I'm a - lone,_

sud - den - ly_ my heart_ goes boom._ It's an or - che - stra of
it seems there's more of us_ at home._ It's a mul - ti - tude of

an - gels,_ they're play-ing with_ my_ heart,_ yeah._____
an - gels_ they're play-ing with_ my_ heart,_ yeah._____

Must be talk-ing to an an-gel, must be talk-ing to an an-gel,

must be talk-ing to an an-gel.___ Must be talk-ing to an an-gel,

must be talk-ing to an an-gel, must be talk-ing to an an-gel.___

Must be talk-ing to an an-gel, must be talk-ing to an an-gel,

must be talk-ing to an an-gel.___ Must be talk-ing to an an-gel,

must be talk-ing to an an-gel, must be talk-ing to an an-gel.__

_ No - one on earth_ could feel like

I must be____ hal - lu - zi - nat - ing, watch - ing an - gels

ce - le - brat - ing. Could this be____ re - ac - ti - vat - ing all____ my sen - ses

dis - lo - cat - ing. This must be a strange____ de - cep - tion,

bi - ce - le - stial in - ter - ven - tion. Leav - ing me____ the

re - col - lec - tion____ of____ your hea - ven - ly____ con - nec - tion.

(improvise ad lib.)

I walk in - to____ an emp - ty room,_____ sud - den - ly____ my heart goes

boom._____ It's an or - che - stra of an - gels,____

they're play-ing with my heart, yeah. Da - da - da - da - da - da - da -

-da, da - da, da - da. Da - da - da - da - da - da - da -

-da, da - da, da - da. Yeah.

(improvise ad lib.)

THIS IS THE LIFE
AMY MACDONALD

♩ = 190 | 8 Beat

Leadsound: Flute

Musik & Text: Amy MacDonald
© 2006 Amy Macdonald Limited
Warner/Chappell Music Publishing Limited, London. Reproduced by permission of Faber Music Limited.
All Rights Reserved. International Copyright Secured.

Oh, the wind whist-les down the cold dark street to-night___ and the peo-ple they were danc - ing to the mu-sic vibe.___ And the boys ___ chase the girls with the curls in their hair___ while the shy tor-men-ted youth sit way o-ver there. And the songs,___ they get lou - der, each one bet-ter than be - fore.

And you're sing-ing the songs___ think-ing this is the life.___ And you wake up in the morn-ing and your head feels twice the size. Where you gon - na go? Where you gon-na go? Where you gon-na sleep to-night?___

1. And you're sing-ing the songs

2. Where you gon-na sleep to-night?___

So you're

head-ing down the road in your tax-i for four_ and you're wait-ing out-side Jim-my's front door but

no-bo-dy's in and no-bo-dy's home 'til____ four. So you're sitt-ing there with

noth-ing to do,__ talk-ing a-bout Ro-bert Ri-ger and his mot-ley crew_ and

D.S. al CODA

where you gon-na go, where you gon-na sleep to-night._ And you're sing-ing the songs

And you're sing-ing the songs

__ think-ing this is the life.__ And you wake up in the morn-ing and your head feels twice the

size. Where you gon-na go? Where you gon-na go? Where you gon-na sleep to-night?

1.-3.   4.

__ And you're sing-ing the songs Where you gon-na sleep to-

night?

THIS LOVE
MAROON 5

♩ = 94	Pop Beat
	Leadsound: Saxophone

Musik & Text: James Valentine, Adam Levine, Jesse Carmichael, Ryan Dusick, Mickey Madden
© Copyright 2002 Universal Music Publishing MGB Limited.
All rights in Germany administered by Musik Edition Discoton GmbH (a division of Universal Music Publishing Group).

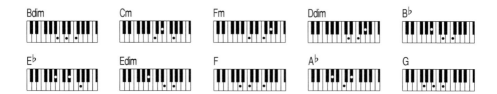

I was so high I did not re - cog - nize, the fi - re burn - ing
I tried my best to feed her ap - pe - tite, keep her co - ming

in her eyes, the cha - os that con - trolled my mind. Whis - pered good - bye and she got
ev' - ry night, so hard to keep her sa - tis - fied. Kept pla - ying love like it was

on a plane, nev - er to re - turn a - gain, but al - ways in my heart.
just a game, pre - ten - ding to feel the same, then turn a - round and leave a - gain. Oh.

This love has ta - ken its toll_ on me, she said good - bye too ma - ny times be - fore.

And her heart is break - ing in front of me, I have no choice 'cause

I won't say good - bye an - y - more._ Oh_ oh oh. Oh_ oh

TIME AFTER TIME
CYNDI LAUPER

♩ = 130   Pop Beat

Leadsound: Flute

Musik & Text: Cyndi Lauper & Robert Hyman
© Copyright Dub Notes Music, Rellla Music Corp.
Für D, A, Ch by Edition Intro Meisel GmbH / Sony/ATV Music Publishing Germany GmbH.
All Rights Reserved. International Copyright Secured.

189

TOXIC
BRITNEY SPEARS

♩ = 143 | 8 Beat

Leadsound: Strings

Musik & Text: Cathy Dennis, Christian Karlsson, Pontus Winnberg & Henrik Jonback

Ba - by, can't you see, I'm call - ing. A guy like you should wear a warn - ing. It's dan - ger - ous, I'm fall - ing.

There's no es - cape, I can't wait. I need a hit, Ba - by, give me it. You're dan - ger - ous, I'm lov - ing it.

Too high, can't come down. Los - in' my head, spin - nin' 'round and 'round.
Too high, can't come down. It's in the air and it's all a - round.

Do you feel me now? With the taste of your lips I'm
Can you feel me now?

on a ride. You're to - xic I'm slip - pin' un - der. Taste of the poi - son

UNIVERSUM
ICH + ICH

♩ = 78 | 8 Beat

Leadsound: Piano

Musik & Text: Annette Humpe
© by Ambulanz Musikverlag Annette Humpe.

Ich weiß, wo-von du träumst
Ich bin glück-lich dich zu sehn.

und meis-tens was du denkst.
Ich will an dir nichts ver-drehn.

Ich kenn dich.___
Ich lass dich.___

Ich seh, ob dich was freut o-der ob es dich kränkt.
Kein Prob-lem in Sicht, was Bess-res gibt es nicht. Ich lass dich, Ich

kenn dich so gut.___
so wie du bist.___

Du hast mehr als je-den Schim-mer von mir.___

Ich weiß, ich häng für im-mer an dir.___ Du kannst in die

Fer-ne flie-gen, durch die Mon-go-lei,___ in tiefs-te Tie-fen tau-chen. Fühl dich frei.__ Das U-ni-

-ver - sum dehnt sich aus. Du kannst die

Gip-fel er-klim-men, zu al-len In-seln schwim-men. In dei-nem

Her - zen bin ich so - wie - so da - bei,__ denn ich bin im - mer dein Zu - haus.__

Gu - te Rei - se, gu - te Rei - se. Ein Jahr ver - geht wie ein Mo - ment.__

Und komm ge - sund_ zu - rück. Gu - te Rei - se, gu - te Rei - se.

Kei - ne Gren - ze, die uns trennt. Und komm ge - sund zu - rück.

Du kannst zu den Ster - nen flie - gen, am O - ri - on vor - bei,__ im Ma - ri -

-an - nen - gra - ben tau - chen, oh, fühl dich frei.__ Das U - ni - ver - sum dehnt sich

aus. Den Mount E - ve - rest er - klim - men, bis nach Is - land schwim - men. In dei - nem

Her - zen bin ich so - wie - so da - bei,__ denn ich bin im - mer dein Zu - haus.__

Ich bin im - mer dein Zu - haus.__

Ich bin im - mer dein Zu - haus.__

VALERIE
MARK RONSON FEAT. AMY WINEHOUSE

♩ = 212 | Pop Beat

Leadsound: Flute

Musik & Text: Dave McCabe, Sean Payne, Abigail Harding, Boyan Chowdhury, Russell Pritchard
© 2006 EMI Music Publishing Limited, London. Reproduced by permission of International Music Publications Limited
(a trading name of Faber Music Limited).
All Rights Reserved.

 Eb
 Fm
 Ab
 Gm
 Bb

Well, some - times I go out___ by my - self,

___ and I look a - cross the wa - ter.___ And I

think of all the things, what you're do - ing and in my head___ I make a pic - ture.___

'Cause since I've come on home, well, my bo - dy's been a mess.___ And I've missed

___ your gin - ger hair___ and the way you like to dress.___

Ah, won't you come on o - ver, stop mak - ing a fool out of me.___

Why won't you come on o - ver, Va - le - rie,___ Va - le - rie,

194

Va - le - rie,__ Va - le - rie._____

Did you have to go to jail, put your house on up for sale, did you get a good

law - yer?__ Hope you did - n't catch a tan, hope you

find the right man__ who'll fix it for you._____ Are you

shop - ping a - ny - where, changed the co - lour of your hair, are__ you bu - sy?

And did you have to pay the fine,__ you were

D.S. al CODA

dod - ging all__ the time,__ are you still diz - zy?_____

Hm,__ Va - le - rie,_____ Va - le - rie,_____

Va - le - rie,_____ Va - le - rie._____ Why

won't you come on o - ver, Va - le - rie._____

195

VIVA LA VIDA
COLDPLAY

♩ = 138 | 8 Beat

Leadsound: Strings

Musik & Text: Guy Berryman, Jon Buckland, Will Champion & Chris Martin
© Copyright 2008 Universal Music Publishing MGB Limited.
All rights in Germany administered by Musik Edition Discoton GmbH (a division of Universal Music Publishing Group).
All Rights Reserved. International Copyright Secured.

cas - tles stand___ up - on pil - lars of salt___ and pil - lars of sand. I

hear Je - ru - sa - lem bells___ are ring - ing, Ro - man ca - val - ry choirs___ are sing - ing.

Be my mir - ror my sword___ and shield,___ my mis - sio - na - ries in a fo - reign field.___

For some rea - son I can't___ ex - plain, once you know there was nev - er, nev - er an hon-

- est word.___ And that was when I___ ruled the world.___

It was the wick - ed and wild

_____ wind___ blew down the doors to let me in.___ Shat - tered win - dows and the

sound_ of drums,___ peo - ple could not be - lieve what I'd___ be - come. Re - vo - lu - tio-

-na - ries wait___ for my head on a sil - ver plate.___ Just a pup - pet on a

lone - ly string.___ Oh, who would e - ver want to be king.___ I

hear Je - ru - sa - lem bells___ are ring - ing, Ro - man ca - val - ry choirs___ are sing - ing.

Be my mir - ror my sword___ and shield,___ my mis - sio - na - ries in a fo - reign field.___

For some rea - son I can't___ ex - plain, I know Saint Pe - ter won't call___ my name nev - er'n

ho - nest word.___ But that was when I___ ruled the world.___

Oh oh oh_ oh oh_____ oh.

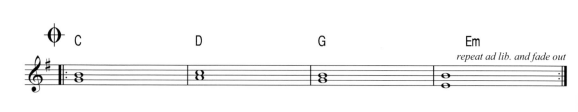

Oh oh oh_ oh oh_____ oh. Oh oh oh_ oh oh I

repeat ad lib. and fade out

WRONG
DEPECHE MODE

♩ = 130	8 Beat
	Leadsound: Synth Lead

Musik & Text: Martin Gore
© 2008 EMI Music Publishing Limited, London. Reproduced by permission of International Music Publications Limited
(a trading name of Faber Music Limited)
All Rights Reserved.

Em

F#m

Bm

G

N.C.

Wrong. Wrong. Wrong.

Em

Wrong. I was born with the wrong sign,_ in the wrong house with the

F#m

wrong as - cen - dan - cy.___ I took the wrong road___ that led to___ the

Bm

wrong ten - den - cies.__ I___ was in the wrong place_ at the wrong time_ for the

G

wrong rea - son and the wrong rhyme. On the wrong day_ of the wrong week,_ I used the

Em

wrong me - thod with the wrong tech - nique. Wrong._

Wrong. There's some-thing wrong with me__ che-mi-cally,__ some-thing wrong with me in-he-rent-ly.__ The wrong mix__ in the wrong genes. I reached the wrong ends__ by the wrong means. It was the wrong plan__ in the wrong hands, the wrong theo - ry for the wrong man.__ The wrong eyes__ on the wrong prize,__ the wrong ques-tions with the wrong re-plies. Wrong. Wrong.

I was march-ing to the wrong drum__ with the wrong scum piss-ing out the wrong e - ner-gy.__ Us-ing all the wrong lines__ and the wrong signs__ with the wrong in-ten - si-ty.__ I__ was on the wrong page__ of the wrong book__ with the

wrong ren - di - tion of the wrong look.__ With the wrong moon,_ ev - 'ry wrong night,_ with the

wrong tune play - ing till it soun - ded right, yeah.____ Wrong.

Wrong. Too long._____ Wrong. Too long._____ Wrong.

Too long._____ Wrong. Too long._____ Wrong.

Too long.__ I was born with the wrong sign__ In the wrong house_ With the

wrong as - cen - dan - cy_____ I took the wrong road__ That led to_____ the

wrong ten - den - cies.__ I___ was in the wrong place_ at the wrong time__ for the

wrong rea - son and the wrong rhyme. On the wrong day_ of the wrong week,_ I used the

wrong me - thod with the wrong tech - nique. Wrong.__

WE ARE THE PEOPLE
EMPIRE OF THE SUN

♩ = 124 | Pop Beat

Leadsound: Vibraphone

Musik & Text: Luke Steele, Nicholas Littlemore & Jonathan Sloan
© Copyright 2009 Sony/ATV Music Publishing / Solola Limited / Universal Music Publishing Limited
(administered in Germany by Universal Music Publishing GmbH).
All Rights Reserved. International Copyright Secured.

can't do well when I think you're gon-na leave me. But I know I try.

Are you gon-na leave me now? Can't you be be-liev-ing now? I
(2.x tacet)

Can you re-mem-ber and hu-ma-nize? It was still where we'd e-ner-gized.

Lie in the sand___ and vi-sua-lize, like it's se-ven-ty-five___ a-gain.

We are the peo-ple that rule the world, a force runn-ing in___ ev'-ry boy and girl.

D.S. al CODA

All re-joic-ing in___ the world. Take me now,___ we can try. I

I know ev-'ry-thing___ ab-out___ you,___ know ev-'ry-thing___ a-bout___ me,___

___ know ev-'ry-thing___ a-bout___ us.___ I

can't do well when I think you're gon-na leave me. But I know I try. Are you gon-na

leave me now? Can't you be be-liev-ing now? I

WE NO SPEAK AMERICANO
YOLANDA BE COOL & DCUP

♩ = 128 | Disco Beat

Leadsound: Saxophone

Text: Nicola Salerno / Musik: Renato Carosone / Arranged by Johnson Peterson, Sylvester Martinez & Duncan MacLennan
© Copyright 1956, 2010 Universal Music Publishing Ricordi SRL, Italy.
Universal Music Publishing MGB Limited. All rights in Germany administered by Musik Edition Discoton GmbH
(a division of Universal Music Publishing Group).
All Rights Reserved. International Copyright Secured.

Pa pa l'a - me - ri - - ca - no!

Pa pa l'a - me - ri - - ca - no!

Pa pa l'a - me - ri -

-ca - no!

Pa pa l'a - me - ri -

Whis - ky,

so - da e rock - 'n' - roll.___ Whis - ky, so - da e rock - 'n' - roll.___ Whis - ky,

so - da e rock - 'n' - roll.___

WEST END GIRLS
PET SHOP BOYS

♩ = 130	Disco Beat
Leadsound: Synth Lead	

Musik & Text: Neil Tennant & Chris Lowe
© Copyright 1985 Cage Music Limited.
Sony/ATV Music Publishing (UK) Limited.
All Rights Reserved. International Copyright Secured.

1.: Sometimes you're better off dead, there's a gun in your hand and it's pointing at your head.
You think you're mad too unstable kicking in chairs and knocking down tables
in a restaurant in a west end town, call the police there's a mad man around.
Running down underground to a dive bar in a west end town.

2.: Too many shadows whispering voices, faces on posters too many choices.
If when why what how much have you got, have you got it, do you get it if so how often,
which do you chose a hard or soft option.

west end town a dead end world, the east end boys and west end girls.

In a west end town a dead end world, the east end boys and

west end girls. West end girls.

West end girls.

In a west end town a dead end world, the east end boys and west end girls.

In a west end town a dead end world, the east end boys and west end girls.

West end girls.

3.: You got a heart of glass or a heart of stone, just you wait till I get you home.
We've got no future, we've got no past, here today built to last.
In every city, in every nation, from Lake Geneva to the Finland station.

In a

west end town a dead end world, the east end boys and west end girls.

In a west end town a dead end world, the east end boys and west end girls.

rep. ad lib.

West end girls.

West end girls.

WHEN LOVE TAKES OVER
DAVID GUETTA FEAT. KELLY ROWLAND

♩= 130 | Disco Beat
Leadsound: Flute

G   Dm   Am   Gsus⁴   F

WHITE FLAG
DIDO

♩ = 85	Pop Beat
Leadsound: Flute	

F   Am   Dm   C   Gm

B♭

1. I know you think that I should-n't still love you, or
2. I know I left too much mess and des-truc-tion to come

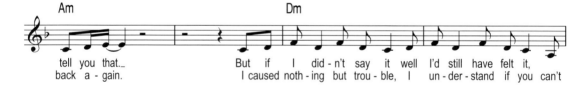

tell you that._ But if I did-n't say it well I'd still have felt it,
back a-gain. I caused noth-ing but trou-ble, I un-der-stand if you can't

where's the sense in that?_ I pro-mise I'm not try-ing to make
talk to me_ a-gain._ And if you live by the rules

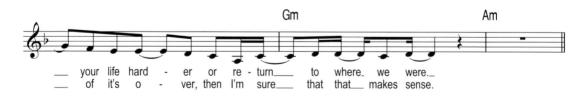

_ your life hard - er or re-turn_ to where_ we were._
_ of it's o - ver, then I'm sure_ that that_ makes sense.

But I will go down with_ this_ ship, and I won't put_ my hands up_ and sur-

Dm   B♭   F   C

-ren - der.   There will be   no white flag a - bove my___ door,   I'm in   love___ and al - ways

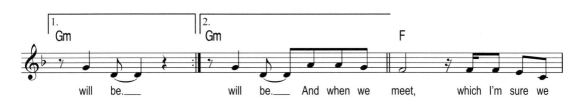

1. Gm   2. Gm   F

will   be.___   will   be.___ And when we   meet,   which I'm sure we

Am   Gm

will.   All that was   there   will be there___ still.   I'll let it   pass_   and hold my_

C

___ tongue,   and you will   think_   that I've_   moved   on._____

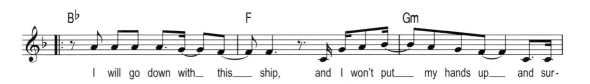

B♭   F   Gm

I will go down with_ this___ ship,   and I won't put___ my hands up___ and sur-

Dm   B♭

-ren - der.   There will be   no   white   flag   a - bove___   my___

F   C   Gm

___ door,   I'm in   love___ and al - ways   will   be.___

WINTER
UNHEILIG

♩= 106 | 8 Beat

Leadsound: Oboe

Musik & Text: Der Graf
© Fansation M.Tombuelt & O. Reimann GbR, Universal Music Publishing GmbH.

Ah. _____ Ah. _____

Streift die Stil - le_ durch die Wäl - der im Traum aus Eis_

_ und Licht._ Liegt der Schnee auf_ Baum und Tä - lern,

strei - cheln Flo - cken_ mein Ge - sicht. Sehnt mein Herz sich nach der Hei -

mat, nach Zu-hau-se,_ Schutz und Halt._ Rückt das Le - ben_ nä - her zu -

sam men,_ spie - geln Träu - me sich_ im Win - ter - land.

Ah. _____ Schneit der Him - mel wei - ße Ster -

- ne._ Ah._ Wer - den Wün sche_ wie - der wahr.

Ah._____ Liegt die Welt im Sil-ber- schnee.

Ah._____ Fängt die Zeit zum Träu-men an._____ *(rep. Refr. on Segno)*

Die Bäu-me stehn in_____ tie-fer Stil-le, der Wind das Ast-

-werk hebt._ Die Kin-der la-chen auf Seen und Bä-chen, der

Frost Schneeb-lu-men an die_____ Fens-ter weht._ Schen-ken Frem-de sich ein Lä-

cheln, rei-chen Men-schen sich die Hand._ Kommt die Welt sich_ et-was nä-

her, spie-geln Träu-me sich_____ im Win-ter- land._

D.S. al CODA

Ah._____

WIRE TO WIRE
RAZORLIGHT

♩ = 116 | Shuffle

Leadsound: Piano

Musik & Text: Johnny Borrell

one you can trust_ to love you,_ a - gain_ and a - gain._

How do you love in a house with - out feel - ings? How do you turn what the

sa - vage take? I've been look - ing for some - one to be - lieve_ in. Love me,_ a -

- gain and a - gain._ She lives_ by dis - il -

-lu- sions close. We go_ where the wild blood flows. On our bo - dies we

share the same scar. How do you love on a

night with - out feel - ings? She says, love, I hear sound, I see fu - ry.

She says, love's not a hos - tile con - di - tion. Love me,_ wher - ev - er you are.

_ Wher - ev - er you are._

215

WONDERFUL LIFE
HURTS

♩ = 120 | Pop Beat
Leadsound: Oboe

Musik & Text: Adam Anderson, Joseph Cross, Theo Hutchcraft
© EMI Music Publishing Limited.
Rechte für Deutschland, Österreich, Schweiz und Osteuropa (außer Baltikum): EMI Music Publishing Germany GmbH /
Printed with kind permission of Big Life Music Limited.

- ing through the cit - y to the tem - ple sta - tion, cries___ in - to the leath - er - seat.

___ And Su - sie knows her ba - by was a fa - mi - liy man,___ but the world

___ has got him down on his knees.___ So she throws___ him at the wall and kis -

- ses burn like fire,___ and sud - den - ly he starts to be - lieve.___ He takes

___ her in his arms and he does - n't know why,___ but he thinks___ that he be - gins___ to see.

___ She says Don't let go! Nev - er give up,___ it's such a

won - der - ful life. Don't let go! Nev - er give up,___ it's such a

won - der - ful life. She says
(only last time)

Don't let go! Nev - er give up___ Don't let go!

Nev - er give up,___ it's such a won - der - ful life.

Don't let go! Don't let go!

YOU KNOW I'M NO GOOD
AMY WINEHOUSE

♩ = 104 | 8 Beat

Leadsound: Saxophone

Musik & Text: Amy Winehouse
© 2006 EMI Music Publishing Limited, London. Reproduced by permission of International Misc Publications Limited
(a trading name of Faber Music Limited).
All Rights Reserved.

Dm   Gm   A   E   F   Am

Meet you down - stairs in the bar and heard your
Up - stairs in bed_ with my ex - boy,_ he's

rolled up sleeves in your skull T - shirt._ You say, "What did you do_ with him_
in the place_ but I can't get joy._ Thin - king on you_ in the

_ to - day?"_ and sniffed me out_ like I was Tan - que - ray._
fi - nal throes,_ this is when_ my_ buz - zer goes._

'Cause you're my fel - la, my guy_ Hand me your
Run out to meet you, chips and pit - ta You say, "When we mar - ried", 'cause

Stel - la and fly._ By the time_ I'm out the door_ you tear men down like
you're not bit - ter. There'll be none_ of him no more, I cried for you on the

Ro - ger Moore. I chea - ted my - self like I knew I would.
kit - chen floor._

_ I told you, I_ was trou - ble._ You know_ that I'm no good.

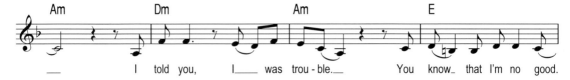

1.
Am
2.
Am
Dm
Am
E
Am
Dm
Sweet re - un - ion Ja -
Gm
A
Dm
mai - ca and Spain, we're like how we were a - gain. I'm in the tub, you
Gm
A
Dm
Gm
on the seat, lick your lips as I soak my feet. And then you no - tice lit - tle
E
F
car - pet burn, my sto - mach drop and my guts churn. You shrug and
E
A
Dm
3
it's the worst. who tru - ly stuck the knife in first. I chea - ted my - self
Am
E
Am
Dm
like I knew I would. I told you, I was
1., 2.
3.
Am
E
Am
Am
trou - ble. You know that I'm no good.
rep. ad lib. and fade out
Dm
Am
E
Am

ZEIG MIR WIE DU TANZT
FRIDA GOLD

♩ = 130	Pop Beat
	Leadsound: Flute

Text: Alina Sueggeler / Musik: Andreas Weizel, Alina Sueggeler

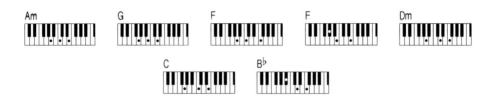

Zeig mir, wie du tanzt, und ich sag dir, wer du bist. Und so wie du guckst, weiß ich, wo-nach dir ist. Zeig mir, wie du sprichst, und ich sag dir, was du hörst. Ich will wis-sen, wie du riechst und ob du mich be-törst. Und so wie du tanzt, kann ich füh-len, wer du bist. Und fast wie in Trance las-sen wir uns drauf ein. Und so wie ich tanz, seh ich's fun-keln in dei-nem Blick. Wir ver-schmel-zen ganz

sanft, fast von_ al - lein. Zeig mir, wie du küsst,

und ich sag dir, ob's mir___ schmeckt. Zeig wie du dich_ be - wegst,

und ob du mei - ne Sin - ne___ weckst. Zeig mir, wie du tanzt - tanzt - tanzt - tanzt,

_____ tanzt - tanzt - tanzt tanzt._____ Zeig mir, wie du tanzt tanzt - tanzt- tanzt.

D.S. al CODA 1

_____ Und ich fühl dich._ Und ich fühl dich. Und so wie_ du

So wie du dich_ be - wegst, macht al - les ei - nen Sinn. So wie du jetzt_ los-

- lässt, kommt plötz - lich al - les hin. So wie du dich an - fühlst, so fühlt sich le - ben

1.

an. Und dich nicht mehr_ auf - führst, so kommst du end - lich an. So wie du dich_ be-

2.

D.S. al CODA 2

- führst so kommst du end - lich an Und so wie_ du Fast von_ al - lein.

221